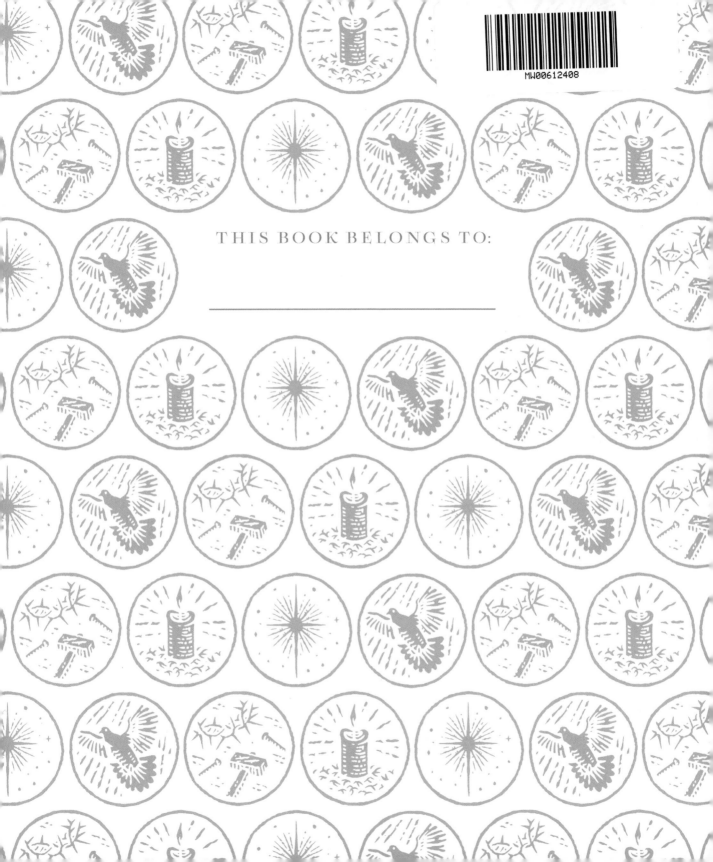

THIS BOOK BELONGS TO:

_____

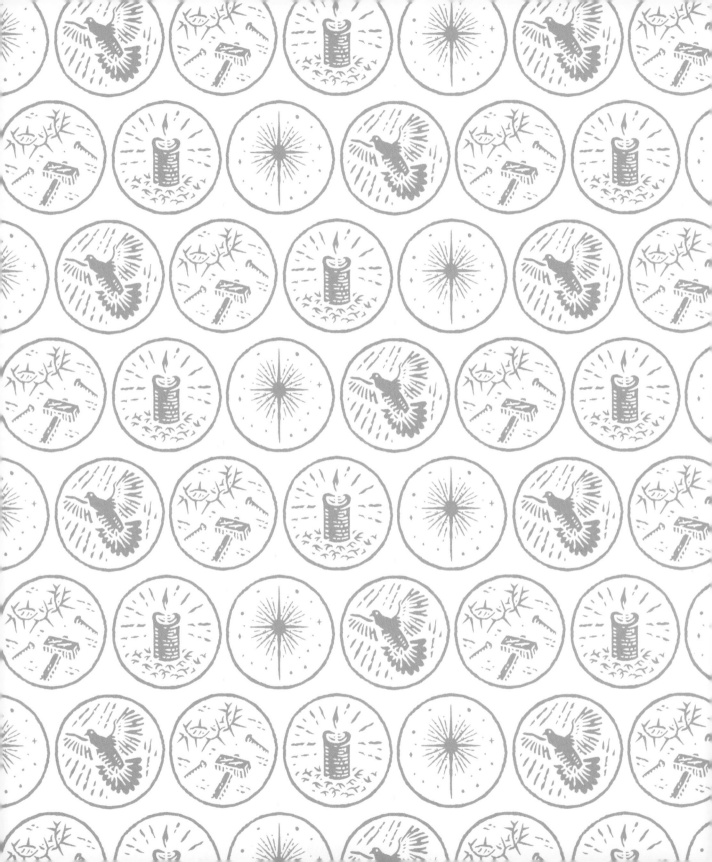

"*Sacred Seasons* makes a warm, winning, and above all practical introduction to the traditional church year, and will be a boon for all who are rediscovering this forgotten treasure of the church, this neglected pattern for Christian living. This book will especially appeal to those who'd like to 'live the liturgy' in a natural way, together, at home, as a family. Wonderful seasonal recipes are interwoven with helpful explanations of the reasons for the seasons and creative ideas for celebrating them together. I am glad to commend this book."

—Rev. Dr. Malcolm Guite, poet and Life Fellow of Girton College, University of Cambridge

"One of the more cheering elements of recent evangelical thought has been a renewed attentiveness to spiritual disciplines, the church year, and the rituals of ordinary Christian piety. If you have read Dallas Willard, John Mark Comer, or Tish Warren and found something valuable in their emphasis on the ordinary practices of Christian discipleship, then *Sacred Seasons* is the practical manual you need to help you incorporate these values into your daily routines. Danielle's book is the best guide I have seen for how to actually begin adopting the practices that have anchored God's people for centuries and helped give flesh to the theological claims of Christian faith."

—Jake Meador, editor in chief of Mere Orthodoxy

"Danielle is a thoughtful teacher whose invitational spirit will help you learn and grow alongside your family as you journey through the liturgical year. This deeply rooted offering is informational yet accessible, historical yet approachable. The spiritual rhythms, routines, and rituals in this artful collection are sure to resource families for years to come."

—Kayla Craig, author of *To Light Their Way* and creator of the *Liturgies for Parents* podcast

"As late converts to liturgical rhythms, the Church Calendar confronted decades of being shaped by school calendars, sports seasons, and a few fun-but-frenzied holidays. Challenging at first, this new way of telling time offered a far more profound way to build the shared rhythms we need as humans. This book is a beautifully crafted sourcebook for shaping our traditions by the awareness that time has been redeemed by Christ. Happily, it's never too late to dig deeper with friends and family. My wife and I look forward to using Danielle Hitchen's gift to shape our coming days more richly than ever, after the greatest story of all."

—Bishop Steven A Breedlove, Diocese of Christ Our Hope, Anglican Church in North America

"If you are looking for a new rhythm for your own personal study, or if you need a fresh plan to help the Scriptures come alive for your children, this book is for you! In this friendly layout you will find nuggets on church history, practical ideas for your kids or grandkids, recipes to make together, and much more. It's a great gift for a young family!"

—Susan Alexander Yates, speaker and author of *Risky Faith*

"This is a beautiful, invigorating, one-of-a-kind book. In an age of praise songs and fog machines, retrieving the church calendar can feel like little more than nostalgic play-acting. Yet the liturgical rhythms have provided a firm anchor for Christian devotion throughout the centuries. Danielle Hitchen has provided a rich treasure to the church in this historically informed, immensely practical how-to guide that offers us baby steps back into spiritual disciplines and promises to root us more deeply in God's grace and communion with our fellow saints."

—Bradford Littlejohn, president of the Davenant Institute

"In *Sacred Seasons*, Danielle Hitchen equips us to place ourselves inside God's story by embracing the often-overlooked liturgical calendar. *Wow!* She has me totally convinced of its value for my family and my faith! She offers approachable, meaningful, and exciting ways for Christians to 'keep time with the Lord' so that God's story informs theirs. Every page captivated my attention, and I am looking forward to inviting these practices to captivate my calendar."

—**Caroline Saunders, author of** *The Story of Water*

"Sacred Seasons offers a biblical, historical, and practical roadmap for living out your faith every day of the year. This book isn't about adding more to your already busy life. Rather, it's about attuning our lives to what God has done and is doing throughout the history of the church. Whether you're familiar with following the church calendar or the concept is completely new, this book is an invaluable resource to help you and your family embody the grand and beautiful story of our redemption."

—**Sarah J. Hauser, speaker and author of** *All Who Are Weary*

"There is nobody I trust more than Danielle Hitchen to help lead my family through the rhythms of discipleship. In *Sacred Seasons*, you'll find a knowledgeable, humble, and encouraging conversation partner, fellow parent, and trustworthy friend. For the parent who has heard of the church calendar but has no clue where to begin, this is your new go-to resource. For the family who has dabbled in church calendar resources, this book will guide you deeper. With a grateful heart, I commend this book to your family and pray that God will use it to bind your heart to his."

—**Chris Ammen, founder of Kaleidoscope Kids' Bibles**

"More than any resource I know, *Sacred Seasons* makes following the Christian calendar approachable *and* enjoyable. This book is meticulously researched and theologically robust—it will be an enormous blessing to anyone who wants to enter more deeply into the rhythms of grace God has given his church."

—**Matthew Lee Anderson, author and founder of Mere Orthodoxy**

"*Sacred Seasons* stirs my longing to experience something bigger than the personal relationship with Christ I know so well. I have often looked for new ways to consistently connect my kids to God through the year—not for the sake of tradition, but so my whole family can grow a deeply rooted faith. As it turns out, the global, millennia-spanning church has the sacred seasonal practices I've been searching for. Danielle reminds us that it's never too late to tune our lives to the melody and rhythms of the church calendar. I'm delighted to discover I'm invited, too, and I'm grateful that she has written the comprehensive, practical guide this mom needed."

—**Christie Thomas, author of** *Fruit Full*

"Sacred Seasons is an incredible gift. It demystifies the church calendar for young families, inviting them into the beauty of orienting our rhythms and routines around Christ and his church. No longer will observing the church calendar with your kids feel too sophisticated or complicated. Danielle has done all the heavy lifting for parents with full arms, from simple liturgies to delicious doable recipes. An accessible must-have for families seeking to make the rhythms of remembrance part of the heartbeat of their home."

—**Abbey Wedgeworth , author of** *Held*

SACRED SEASONS

DANIELLE HITCHEN

ART BY STEPHEN CROTTS

HARVEST HOUSE PUBLISHERS
EUGENE, OREGON

For my Lord.
Take my moments and my days,
let them flow in ceaseless praise.

For everything there is a season, and a time for every matter under heaven:
a time to be born, and a time to die;
a time to plant, and a time to pluck up what is planted;
a time to kill, and a time to heal;
a time to break down, and a time to build up;
a time to weep, and a time to laugh;
a time to mourn, and a time to dance;
a time to cast away stones, and a time to gather stones together;
a time to embrace, and a time to refrain from embracing;
a time to seek, and a time to lose;
a time to keep, and a time to cast away;
a time to tear, and a time to sew;
a time to keep silence, and a time to speak;
a time to love, and a time to hate;
a time for war, and a time for peace.

ECCLESIASTES 3:1-8

CONTENTS

ACKNOWLEDGMENTS

I am overwhelmingly grateful to the community of people who have supported this book from inception to hard copy. I would, however, be remiss if I failed to specifically acknowledge several individuals. Without these people, *Sacred Seasons* wouldn't exist:

To my husband, Nathan, for being with me and for me, for your words of encouragement, and for the sacrifice of your time, thank you.

Mom and Dad, for your love for my children and for the gift of your quiet basement to write in, I am ever grateful.

Alice, Charlie, and Eleanor, thank you for your patience, forbearance, and sharing me so often with my laptop. For your trouble, your names are in a book!

Jay and Frances, may the Lord bless you for your hospitality and granting me a space in which to birth this manuscript.

Shannon, Ashley, Elizabeth, Meagan, Joanna, Annie, and Marissa, for listening to me talk endlessly about this book (and continuing to graciously ask me, "How's it going?"), thank you. Your friendship is a gift.

Ashley, my girl Friday, this manuscript would have been in shambles without you–thank you for being willing to do a thousand little tasks to make this book a reality.

Andrew, if you have half as much patience for your children as you do for me, you're a tremendous dad. Thank you for being the World's Best Agent.

Kyle, for inviting my thoughts on this topic and for being really good at your job, I will be forever grateful. And to the whole Harvest House team, thank you for taking a chance on this project and for your tremendous work to bring it to fruition.

INTRODUCTION

Our table is laid with a deep purple runner, and two tapers gently flicker in the Advent wreath at the center. After silencing the record player, my husband dims the overhead lights. Our three children gather around to light the third candle. Opening my Bible, I begin to read the appointed Scripture lessons for the third Sunday of Advent.

"Mom!" my three-year-old whisper-shouts.

I continue reading.

"Esuse me, Mom!" she persists.

"Yes?" I ask with as much patience as I can.

"Can I bo out the candos now?"

As Advent begins each year, I envision this moment with a soft glow, my children's faces lit with anticipation and candlelight, the smell of ginger-spiced cookies wafting in from the kitchen. The reality is more earthy—someone hops up in the middle of prayer to use the bathroom, we get a long-winded anecdote about Wild Kratts that was sparked by something tenuously related to the reading, and in the end, the best part of the evening for my kids is blowing out the candles.

In spite of all that, there is an ordinary beauty to these moments. However irreverently they may be observed by a family of young kids, the sacred liturgies of the church year, sometimes called the Cycle of Grace, patiently invite us into something deeper, something permanent and eternal. In them, we slow down and pivot our focus—for a few seconds at least—to snatch a glimpse of God's largeness, our own smallness, and the gift of being welcomed into his glorious kingdom.

As the people of God, we are the keepers of this gospel—of *the* gospel. We are the great bards who rehearse and perform the drama of the great story of God's kingdom from creation to second coming. We do this implicitly in the way we live our lives and explicitly in our worship. This story reflects the highs and lows and middles of our own lived experience. It shapes us, giving us definition and depth, containing our beginning and our end, and informing how we live in the in-between. It is a story that should be as familiar to us as our own heartbeat, a tale we inhabit like a fish in the ocean—tiny in comparison to its vastness, but completely at home there anyway.

My awareness of my own place in this story started in college when my studies sparked a curiosity about the historic forms of Christian worship. It was in my local church that I had my first glimpses of the rhythms of the church year—the shrouded cross during Lent, the changing vestment colors, but I *really* remember Easter. The joy! The utter transformation of our worship from a time of quiet penitence to glorious celebration! I was keen to learn more, to dive deeper, to discover the riches I suspected awaited me if only I stepped toward them.

And so I did. Year by year, practicing the ancient rhythms of the church calendar made new grooves in my spirit, habituating me to organize my year and my family's life around the life of Christ.

As my children get older, I see how these practices that began as fun novelties are becoming meaningful. Each year they look forward to pulling out our Advent candles, ask when we will get ashes and put up the paper chain to count down to Easter, and enthusiastically wear their reddest clothes on Pentecost. And each year they draw more connections between the big story of Scripture and our traditional prayers, songs, and activities.

Though the church year can (and should!) be enjoyed by people of all ages, stages, and walks with the Lord, I have written this book specifically with families in mind. The church year is such a simple and natural way to call children into the life of Christ. Kids love liturgies! And rituals! And traditions! The prayers said week after week, the stories read year by year, and the traditions developed with each annual cycle naturally and deeply ingrain God's big story into their little consciousnesses.

So I invite you and your families to join me and mine in observing the ancient liturgies and traditions of the church, participating in faithful remembrance and recitation of God's story.

May the Spirit shape us through these rhythms—however unlike my softly glowing vision they may look—as we seek to honor the Lord with our time.

May we catch a glimpse of what God is doing in the life of his people and rejoice to be counted among them.

And may the sacred seasons of the Cycle of Grace teach us to be ever more at home in God's glorious kingdom.

Amen.

PART ONE

IN HIS TIME

Our times are in your hands:
> But we count our times for us;
>> we count our days and fill them with us;
>> we count our weeks and fill them with our busyness;
>> we count our years and fill them with our fears.

And then caught up short with your claim,
> Our times are in your hands!

Take our times, times of love and times of weariness,
Take them all, bless them and break them,
> give them to us again,
>> slow paced and eager,
>> fixed in your readiness for neighbor.
> Occupy our calendars.
> Flood us with itsy-bitsy, daily *kairoi*,
> in the name of your fleshed *kairos*. Amen.

WALTER BRUEGGEMANN, "OCCUPY OUR CALENDARS"

KEEP SACRED TIME

The liturgical calendar as a whole exists in large part to remind us that Christ has sanctified all of time, bringing us and the whole of our experience into the orbit of resurrection.

LAURENCE HULL STOOKEY, *CALENDAR: CHRIST'S TIME FOR THE CHURCH*

Do you keep a planner or a Google calendar?

Do you worship on Sundays?

Do you celebrate birthdays?

You are a timekeeper. Jammed between birth and death, time is a universal and inescapable element of the human experience.

Aside from the "significant" dates, our daily time—ordinary time, if you will—exerts an enormous influence in our lives. Most of our time is spent doing things that are perfectly routine. On average, humans spend…

26 years sleeping,

13 years working,

8.3 years watching television,

4.5 years eating,

126 days waiting in line,

15 days laughing.[1]

And these are the things that define us. As Annie Dillard famously said, "How we spend our days is, of course, how we spend our lives."[2] Human identity and functioning are completely dependent on timekeeping.

God in Time, Time in Us

In Scripture, there are two basic notions of time: *kairos* and *chronos. Chronos* is just what it sounds like: chronological, ordered time (days, weeks, years). *Kairos* is God's opportune time, the "right moment," the divine intersection of *chronos* and eternity. While God is not subject to the limitations of time (*chronos*), he absolutely works in time to bring forth his *kairos*.

Genesis 1–3 reveals that this intersection of time and eternity is an intentional part of God's design for his creation. Temporal creation (man) walked and talked with eternity himself (God) in Eden. At the fall, the easy relationship between the two was utterly fractured and time became a vehicle for decay and death. To remedy this, Galatians 4:4 explains, "When *the fullness of time* had come, God sent forth his Son" (emphasis added). God's desire is to bring eternity to bear on temporality, fully redeeming the time.

When God—at the incarnation—humbled himself to become subject to the material realities of time (decay, death), he exalted humanity—at the resurrection—to have access to eternal life. The good news of the gospel is not only our redemption from sin but also our restoration to eternity (John 3:16). In this restoration, God has made us inheritors of his work, and the keepers of *sacred time.*

By honoring sacred time, we bear witness to all God has done, is doing, and will do. In Genesis 1, God establishes the sacred cycles of day, week, and year. Each is rooted in Jewish tradition and reinterpreted by Christ's resurrection. Each tells a distinct story about who God is. Each keeps us firmly ensconced in God's great work. As we continually and consciously participate in these cycles, we learn to better inhabit the wonderful story of our faith.

The Sacred Day

Most people conceptualize the day as being from the moment they wake until the moment they go to sleep. In the technical sense, a day is understood as lasting from 12:00 a.m. to 11:59 p.m. But over the first six days of creation, Genesis 1 repeatedly describes the day: "There was evening and there was morning." Because of these words, the Jewish people believed that when it was dark enough for three stars to have appeared in the sky, one day was ended, another begun.

Evening is best understood as the onset of God's creative work and the ceasing of our own. Eugene Peterson writes, "The Hebrew evening/morning sequence conditions us to the rhythms of grace.... Evening: God begins, without our help, his creative day. Morning: God calls us to enjoy and share and develop the work he initiated."[3] Indeed, Peterson indicates that the proper posture upon waking is that of someone who is jumping into the middle of a project. We ask God, "What can we do to help you today?" rather than, "Here's *my* plan for the day—please help?" God is always the initiator in our work, providing the context and meaning to our efforts.

Each day creation preaches the gospel to us afresh—from the largeness of the rising sun to the smallness of our own waking bodies. We can no more prevent Christ's resurrection power from transforming the world than we can prevent the sun from rising each morning to light the earth! As we wake, we can joyfully and consciously enter into the redemptive rhythm of the day, recognizing the daily gift of resurrection life and offering a commencement prayer: "Arise, my soul, arise! / Stretch forth to things eternal."[4]

The Sacred Week

The weekly rhythm of work and rest is also rooted in our history as the people of God, and freshly interpreted by the resurrection. When Jesus walked out of the tomb, behold, his people were made new (2 Corinthians 5:17). With the resurrection, Christ inaugurated the promised and long-awaited new creation, allowing us to inhabit—however incompletely—the final Sabbath: rest from sin and death. In the history of the church, Sunday is sacred because it is the day Christ was resurrected from the grave and thus the day of our own resurrection in him. As such, each Sunday of the year is considered a mini-Easter—a day of great joy and celebration.

When we gather to worship on Sunday each week, we share in Christ's resurrected life and celebrate our entry into the final Sabbath. As new creations in Christ, we access God's ultimate Sabbath rest—we are no longer burdened by the intolerably heavy yoke of sin but are free to live in the power of the Holy Spirit. We *rest always* under the light and easy yoke of Jesus. Our worship is transformed by the Spirit into a foretaste of the coming kingdom, a glimpse of the glorious final intersection of heaven and earth, the fully realized rest in the presence of God.[5]

EIGHTH DAY OF CREATION

Because it is the dawn of new creation, Sunday is also known as the eighth day of creation. While seven is the biblical number of completion, eight is the number of redemption.[6] But the first and the eighth day are, in fact, the same day, which reveals something true about God's work: It's harmonious. Laurence Hull Stookey explains: "As the eighth note of the [musical] scale is consonant with but higher than the first, so the new creation does not demean the creation of the cosmos, but reveals to us fuller insights into the Creator's purpose and providence."[7] As those made new by the resurrection, we participate more fully in the first creation, illuminating the contours of what it was always intended to be: an open, loving relationship between Creator and created.

The Sacred Year

If you ask anyone about the annual traditions of the church, most people go straight to Christmas and Easter. A few may mention Advent and Palm Sunday, or perhaps the much-beloved summer VBS. (I'm sorry to say, vacation Bible school is not an official part of the liturgical year.) These popular holidays are certainly centerpieces of the sacred year; much of what we celebrate pivots on these special days.

Like our days and weeks, the church's annual cycle was inspired by the yearly rhythm of the ancient Israelites. God commanded the Jewish people to observe seven annual feasts. Each feast rehearsed the story of God's redemptive love, pressing the community to remember God's character, faithfulness, and miraculous work. They were called to experience the story for themselves anew every year and teach their children to do the same. These annual celebrations were designed as opportunities for Israel to gather as a community and bring the Lord's work to life once again.

While the Christian liturgical calendar does not have a one-to-one correspondence with the Jewish holy days, it functions in the same way: It anchors us in God's great story, calling us to remember together the work God has done for us.

Structured according to the life of Christ, the church calendar contains six distinct seasons, which are intended to reflect the arc of redemptive history. It runs in two cycles of preparation, celebration, and proclamation:

THE CYCLE OF LIGHT
Advent, Christmas, Epiphany

THE CYCLE OF LIFE
Lent, Easter, Ordinary Time

Each season reflects a distinct piece of Jesus's life or the life of God's people, and each has unique themes, disciplines, and traditions to facilitate growth in the life of faith.

The church year guides us in a yearlong meditation on God's redemptive love. Every 365 days, we journey through the history of God's people, the life of Christ, and the work of the Holy Spirit. As we do so, the church calendar rightly places us within God's story, reminding us that our own birth is not the start of the story—it is only our entrance into *the* story. Intentionally living the annual rhythms of the church year is an excellent way to participate in the life of Christ. This way of experiencing time allows us to tailor our life to our faith, rather than jamming our faith into our life. Christ becomes the center of our calendar, and our lives are formed by and with and in him.

As we orient our day to the work of God, our week to the resurrection, and our year to redemptive history, these rhythms of sacred time fundamentally reform our identity as the people of God, enabling us to embody the gospel in every season. Living in alignment to God's big story is one of the best ways to disciple ourselves and our children. When we walk alongside him in this manner, we habituate not just our minds but also our hearts and bodies to live as Christ's own.

TRAIN FOR RIGHTEOUSNESS

You have made us for yourself, and our hearts are restless until we find our rest in you.

<small>SAINT AUGUSTINE, *CONFESSIONS*</small>

While Christians would ideally be formed by Christ alone, we are unfortunately still fallen, subject to sin and death, and therefore susceptible to being shaped by less desirable influences. In his book *You Are What You Love*, James K.A. Smith describes how cultural rituals form us, explaining that human beings are fundamentally lovers and so are most shaped by what we do, because we *do* what we *love*.[1] Ultimately, what you love, what you spend your time doing, is what you worship. So we must learn to worship well, taking care how we spend our time and where we direct our love and desire.

We can't, however, think our way into virtue and holiness. We often know the theory but fail the practicum. But if you are what you worship, then the most fundamental question is, *how* do we worship, love, and keep time with the Lord such that we become formed by and into his character?

When someone says, "Tell me about yourself," what comes to mind first? The things you want to share (or *not* share) are indicative of how you spend your time, what you love, and what you worship.

Practice Spiritual Disciplines

The practice of spiritual disciplines is the foundation of becoming a disciple of Christ. In the common vernacular, the word *discipline* is often used to indicate punishment or correction. But in Hebrews 12:10 the Greek word for discipline (*paideia*) actually denotes education. When we talk about the discipline of God, we should think of it as instruction rather than reprimand.

This education goes beyond mere head knowledge. Righteousness requires *practice*. Paul writes in 1 Timothy 4:7, "Train yourself for godliness." The word *train* here is *gymnaze*—it's an action verb about conditioning our bodies and building our muscles. Spiritual discipline is the whole-self training that facilitates spiritual growth, building the muscles of righteous living and conforming us into the image of Christ. These habits are encouraged in Scripture as a means of cultivating faith. By the power of the Holy Spirit, the spiritual disciplines transmute our head knowledge into heart knowledge, our instruction into habits.

If we want to be conformed to the image of Christ, then we must *spend time doing* the things that Jesus did:

- He practiced prayer, solitude, and silence, routinely desiring time away to be with his Father.
- He prayed with and for others.
- He fasted (forty days in the wilderness).
- He served others.
- He went regularly to the temple and synagogue for communal worship and to learn the Scriptures (Luke 2:41-52).
- He kept sacred time, remembering the Sabbath as well as the Jewish calendar of feasts.

These are the spiritual disciplines. If you want to be like Jesus, *do these things*. These habits formed the rich inner life of Christ that shaped his visibly abundant outer life.

By these practices he was so deeply connected to the Father, so incredibly attuned to the Holy Spirit, that he was able to resist the temptations of sin and walk in obedience to the Father's will. If we also want to share in Christ's abundant life, we must *do these things*.

Being intentional about spiritual disciplines is not to encourage works righteousness or earning your place in the kingdom. Spiritual disciplines are *not* a requirement for the forgiveness of sins or the hope of heaven. But the gospel is not only forgiveness of sins (justification) but also the promise of abundant, eternal life in Christ (sanctification). By these practices—Scripture, prayer, service, worship, fasting, feasting, and remembering sacred time—we become sanctified. Paul writes in Romans 6:4 that we have been raised with Christ to "walk in newness of life." The spiritual disciplines are a way we access abundant life, enabling us to live as redeemed people who are empowered by the Holy Spirit, ever responding to God's grace, and seeking to conform to Christ's image.

Jesus says, "I came that they may have life and have it abundantly."

JOHN 10:10

The Church Calendar Is a Spiritual Discipline

The overarching spiritual discipline of the liturgical year is *remembering*. Jesus kept sacred time by remembering the Sabbath and the Jewish holy days. In fact, he was celebrating Passover the night he was arrested! Instead of spending his last hours healing, preaching to crowds, or serving the poor, he made the ritual sacrifice of the Passover lamb at the temple and enjoyed the hallowed meal with his closest friends. In this choice, Jesus models the profound significance and necessity of *remembering* God's work—not merely in his head but in his heart and with his actions.

While we often use *remember* colloquially to describe the act of keeping in mind important tasks—feeding the pets, picking up the kids, ensuring we sent a birthday card to Mom—the biblical sense of remembrance is richer. It's more akin to the idea of *experiencing again* or *bringing to life*. To "dismember" something is to take it apart; to "remember" is to pull something back together, to draw it into yourself and make it your own "member." The Greek word for this is *anamnesis*; Patricia Buckland explains that as early Christians observed holy days, they "not only called an event into mind but also into being."[2] In our own celebration of the church year, we are called to make the exceptional past work of God present in our own time and place, in our own hearts and lives. And year after year, through this remembrance, God's work is accomplished.

Furthermore, our present celebrations are shaped not only when we bring God's past into our present but also when we bring God's *future* into our present (the Greek for this is *prolepsis*). We encounter both when we take Communion. The act of partaking of the bread and wine is simultaneously an experience of Jesus's death on the cross and the wedding feast of the Lamb who is to come. These pieces of past and future collide in our present, giving us a brief (and literal) taste of *kairos* by the power of the Holy Spirit.

The Cycles of Light and Life also invite us, by *anamnesis* and *prolepsis*, into experiences of *kairos*:

- In acknowledging that Jesus has already come and will come again, his coming is made present in our own lives.
- In celebrating the historic resurrection and looking forward to our final, physical resurrection, we presently experience the resurrection as new creations in Christ.

In *remembering*—making present—God's past and his future, we are transformed by the Holy Spirit into walking, talking intersections of time and eternity: embodiments of the gospel.

LIVE THE LITURGY

The liturgy of the Church seeks to relate all time to the redemptive purpose of God, giving it meaning in time and in eternity.

PHILIP H. PFATTEICHER, *JOURNEY INTO THE HEART OF GOD: LIVING THE LITURGICAL YEAR*

The practice of spiritual disciplines was born out of a desire to equip those who put their faith in Christ and help them mature in the knowledge and love of the Lord. Over the centuries, as the church sought to help its people conform to the image of Christ, practices called liturgies were put into place. The liturgies used by the church today are the tried-and-true rituals of two millennia of orthodox Christian worship. These are habits and practices designed to help us effectively do the things Christ did.

Liturgy comes from two Greek words—*leitos*, meaning "public," and *ergon*, meaning "to work." The Greek mashup is *leitourgia*, which means "work for the people" or "work of the people." Jesus, in the Great Commission, clearly explains the *leitourgia* of his church: "Go therefore and make disciples of all nations, baptizing them in the name of the Father and of the Son and of the Holy Spirit, teaching them to observe all that I have commanded you" (Matthew 28:19-20). By the power of the Holy Spirit, the church is equipped to do both the work *of* the people (evangelism) and the work *for* the people (discipleship).

Christian liturgy is drawn from Israel's past, reinterpreted in light of the resurrection, and enacted with an orientation toward our future hope. Christian liturgical structures are continually rehearsing the work God has already done, reminding us of the power of Christ within us, and pointing us to the day when God will finally make all things new.

Taking its cue from the Jewish practices of the temple, the early church built the first liturgy around teaching, fellowship, Eucharist (or Communion), and prayer (Acts 2:42). As Christianity grew and spread, it had to become more organized and streamlined to maintain orthodoxy across thousands of miles, thousands (then millions) of people, and thousands of years. Remember, the printing press wasn't invented until around AD 1440. Books—including the Bible—had to be meticulously copied by hand. Most people were illiterate and could not afford their own Bible even if they could read. Liturgy is a way to transmit orthodox belief and practice to many people, in many places, over a great deal of time.

The liturgy of the church includes what James K.A. Smith describes as "faithful innovation."[1] While it started with formalizing traditions Jesus commanded (the Lord's Supper and baptism), it also drew on Jewish and cultural customs to establish rhythms of church life (service structures, prayers, Scripture memory, holy days, and so on). Over the last 2,000 years, the body of Christ has "continued to discern the scripts that should characterize a worshipping community centered on the ascended Christ who prayed for kingdom come."[2]

As the church grew, the liturgy likewise became more structured to support Christians seeking to mature in faith. Church services came to include scripted prayers, Scripture readings, confession and absolution, hymns, making peace with one another, preaching the Word, and Communion. The liturgy expanded to include the observance of holy days—baptism celebrations, days of fasting and feasting, seasons for especially remembering the resurrection and the birth of Christ. The liturgy extended to structures for helping Christians cultivate their relationship with the Lord during the week, especially rubrics for prayer and Scripture meditation. If these sound like spiritual disciplines, it's because they are! The liturgy took the regular activities of Jesus's life and gave them form and structure so they could be effectively taught and replicated over space and time.

The liturgies of the church matter. Christian historian Jaroslav Pelikan famously wrote, "Tradition is the living faith of the dead, traditionalism is the dead faith of the living. And, I suppose I should add, it is traditionalism that gives tradition such a bad name."[3] As twenty-first-century worshippers, we have the great privilege of walking in the beautiful and vibrant traditions of two millennia of faithful believers. May we respect their wisdom.

The Calendar

The church calendar, like all the church's liturgies, is a communal event. We join with our brothers and sisters throughout space and time to remember and honor the work God has already done for us through Christ, is still doing for us through the Holy Spirit, and will do for us at the end of time.

As we commemorate in real time with one another, we also draw courage from the saints who came before. Christians have been remembering holidays on the church calendar for more than a thousand years—or in the case of Easter, nearly 2,000 years! Each time we participate in a church-observed feast or fast, we are—to quote the Apostles' Creed—joining with the communion of saints. From faithful Israelites who crossed the Jordan River to the apostles of Jesus to the people sitting next to us in the pews on Sunday, we are one body, celebrating what God has done for us, living in the light of his truth, and looking with hope to our final resurrection.

A TIMELINE OF THE CHURCH CALENDAR

A timeline of the development of all the church's liturgies is, unfortunately, a project for a totally different book, but here's a quick look at how the calendar developed over time.

Mid- to late first century— Easter established as an annual feast; Lent established as a forty-hour fast preceding Easter

Late second century— Epiphany celebrated formally in the Eastern church as the Feast of the Baptism of Christ

Late second century—Easter established (in some regions)

as a fifty-day feast celebrating the resurrection, ascension, and Pentecost

Early third century—Lent established as a forty-day fast; Ember Days begin to be observed in the West

Early to mid-third century— Holy Week traditions established in Jerusalem

AD 325—Easter "fixed" on being held the first Sunday after the first full moon after the vernal (spring) equinox on March 21 (at the Council of Nicaea)

AD 336—Earliest formal records of Christmas celebrations in the Western church; Feast of the Holy Cross established in the Eastern church

The Sanctoral Calendar

There is a second church calendar known as the "Sanctoral Cycle" or Calendar of Saints. *Saint* comes from the Latin *sanctus*, meaning "holy," and the word *saint* is the noun form of the verb *consecrated*. This term is used to describe all those who have been set apart for the Lord. To be a saint is both to acknowledge the present reality of our new identity in Christ and to inspire us to be worthy of the name.

As inheritors of the kingdom of heaven, we are also inheritors of the great lineage of the saints, our faithful brothers and sisters in Christ. Hebrews 12:1-2 says it best: "Therefore, since we are surrounded by so great a cloud of witnesses, let us also lay aside every weight, and sin which clings so closely, and let us run with endurance the race that is set before us, looking to Jesus." We run with our eyes on Christ, but also encircled and bolstered by the faithful who have gone before us and who currently run beside us.

The saints we remember as a part of the Sanctoral Calendar are people who have been marked out as having an especially great witness. These are "people like us who by the power of the Holy Spirit have lived the new life here and who now support and encourage us in our present struggle to be faithful to our baptismal calling."[4]

Late fourth century—The great exchange of feasts: the West adopts Epiphany and the East adopts the Feast of Christ's Nativity

AD 470—Rogation Days established in Vienne, France, and begin to spread regionally

Late sixth century—Advent fixed at four weeks preceding Christmas

AD 609—May 13 established as the Feast of Saint Mary and All Martyrs (eventually All Saints' Day)

Seventh century—Feast of the Holy Cross added to the Western church calendar

Late eighth century—Rogationtide officially added to the church calendar

AD 835—All Saints' Day moved to November 1

AD 1091—Ash Wednesday becomes a participatory event for the whole church

AD 1334—Trinity Sunday officially added to the church calendar

AD 1925—Christ the King Sunday added to church calendar

If you wanted to celebrate a saint's day every day of the year, that would actually be possible. Unfortunately, that's a whole other book's worth of information. In this book, I've tried to detail the days that have the most bearing on the church calendar, the secular calendar, or both. If you want to celebrate more saints, there are usually great ideas on blogs and Pinterest for crafts and snacks to enjoy while you celebrate.

PRAYING TO THE SAINTS

One of the big questions that inevitably comes up in a discussion of saints is...*but do we pray to them?* Within the Protestant tradition, the answer to that question is unequivocally no. As far as we know, the church triumphant possesses no power to grant the requests of the church militant. Scripture does not indicate that we ought to pray to anyone other than God.

A CALENDAR OF (A FEW) SAINTS' DAYS

DECEMBER 6—Saint Nicholas*

DECEMBER 13—Saint Lucy*

DECEMBER 21—Saint Thomas the Apostle

DECEMBER 26—Saint Stephen the Martyr*

DECEMBER 27—Saint John the Evangelist*

DECEMBER 27—The Holy Innocents*

JANUARY 18—Confession of Saint Peter

JANUARY 25—Conversion of Saint Paul

FEBRUARY 14—Saint Valentine*

FEBRUARY 24—Saint Matthias the Apostle

MARCH 17—Saint Patrick*

MARCH 19—Saint Joseph, husband of Mary

APRIL 23—Saint George

APRIL 25—Saint Mark the Evangelist

MAY 1—Saint Philip and Saint James
(son of Alpheus) the Apostles

MAY 30—Saint Joan of Arc

JUNE 11—Saint Barnabas

JUNE 24—Nativity of Saint John the Baptist*

JUNE 29—Saint Peter and Saint Paul the Apostles

JULY 22—Saint Mary Magdalene

JULY 25—Saint James (son of Zebedee) the Apostle

AUGUST 15—Saint Mary the Virgin

AUGUST 24—Saint Bartholomew the Apostle

SEPTEMBER 3—Saint Phoebe the Deacon

SEPTEMBER 21—Saint Matthew the Evangelist

SEPTEMBER 29—Holy Michael and All Angels*

OCTOBER 4—Saint Francis

OCTOBER 18—Saint Luke the Evangelist

OCTOBER 23—Saint James of Jerusalem
(Jesus's brother)

OCTOBER 28—Saint Simon and
Saint Jude the Apostles

NOVEMBER 1—Feast of All Saints*

NOVEMBER 11—Saint Martin of Tours

NOVEMBER 30—Saint Andrew the Apostle

* Additional details about these feasts are included in this book.

PART TWO

THE CHURCH YEAR

ENJOYING THE CHURCH YEAR

*We want to inhabit the still-unfolding Story of God
and have it inhabit and change us.*

BOBBY GROSS, *LIVING THE CHRISTIAN YEAR*

Perhaps by now you are convinced, or at least open to considering, that observing sacred time is a way to honor God, to be more deeply discipled into the life of Christ, and to participate in the rich tradition of the church. The rest of this book is devoted to helping you do just that with a season-by-season look at the church year.

The following chapters examine each season to better understand the ways that each is a microcosm of the whole—how each season places us in God's story, the spiritual disciplines that encourage us to lean into the season's themes, and the communal traditions that allow individuals and families to engage the season. In addition, each chapter includes a liturgy for family prayer and weekly readings.

Before you dive into the next chapters, I have a few housekeeping notes:

Minor feasts of the church year are somewhat out of order. While the liturgical year is theoretically a chronological celebration of the life of Christ, it's also not. For instance, the baptism of Jesus is celebrated alongside the arrival of the magi. There are generally good reasons for the placement of these one-off feasts—don't let the seeming disorder throw you off!

Many pieces of the church year are moveable. This is a little annoying since it means you can't plan on one start date (or end date) for significant events most years. Among the moveable feasts are Easter, Pentecost, and the beginning of Advent. The best way to determine the date of most things on the church calendar is to google "[event name] [year]."

Remember to look ahead. Enjoying the cycles of the church year does require some planning. Read the next season's chapter before that season begins so that you have time to plan the ways you want to participate in it. Note that many of the seasons of the church year *begin* with a significant date or celebration, so if you don't look ahead, you'll be caught unawares!

Many prayers in this book are labeled "collect." A collect is used to gather the intentions of the worshippers and focus their worship. When used to refer to a prayer, the emphasis of that word is on the first syllable instead of the second (pronounced "COL-lect" instead of "col-LECT").

***The Book of Common Prayer* is a guide to worship.** It is a product of the English Reformation originally written in 1549 by Thomas Cranmer. It contains guides for Sunday worship, individual and family prayer, special services, daily and weekly readings, and collects. Over the last 500 years, it has been periodically revised or updated. Many of the liturgies in this book have drawn heavily on *The Book of Common Prayer*.

Tips for Observing the Church Year with Kids

- **Don't do everything every year.** It's too much and you'll burn out quickly. Pick a few activities (or just one) for each season or feast day and let that be enough. Observing the church year is a lifetime project; it's meant for repetition and practice. If you miss something one year, you'll have an opportunity to do it again next year.

- **It's okay to put off minor feast day celebrations.** Let's face it, observing a saint's day in the middle of a week of work or school can be challenging. It's okay to observe the feast a few days after it's assigned date.

- **It's not always going to go how you planned.** There will be years when you burn the hot cross buns. Or when your kid just doesn't *like* the hot cross buns. Or when they're more like hot mess buns. Or when you don't even bake them. Take a breath and let it go. While you may be disappointed by the outcome of your efforts (or lack thereof), there's always next year. Seek what the Lord has for you in that moment, and move on to the next one in his grace.

- **The church year is for *you* too.** Maybe you can't pull off a giant waffle dinner for the Feast of the Annunciation this year. Maybe you don't even tell your kids it *is* the Feast of the Annunciation this year. That doesn't mean *you* can't sit in Luke 1 for a few minutes, praying through faithfulness in parenting and being encouraged by Mary's obedience.

Just a final reminder that *it's worth making the effort*. I know it's a lot of extra work to fill their shoes on Saint Nicholas Day or bake the special treat during an already full week, but when you facilitate a special celebration or remembrance, you are making family memories in addition to making disciples. Your efforts are not in vain.

Family Liturgy

In each chapter, there is a liturgy intended for family use. It was written to be enjoyed weekly (though it can easily be adapted for daily use). It includes:

- The season's memory verse
- An opening antiphon—a verse or phrase prayed in call-and-response
- A weekly or daily scripture reading (You could also swap in readings from your favorite storybook Bible.)
- A seasonal hymn
- Prayer (the Lord's Prayer and the closing prayer)

If one piece of this doesn't work for your family, skip it. If the seasonal closing prayer is all you can manage with your kids right now, just do that. Don't let the perfect be the enemy of the good. Any investment in the spiritual life of your children is an investment well made. Plant the seeds—however small—and let the Lord give the growth.

Final Reminders

Visually, the liturgical year is represented by a circle (you can see how each season fits into a glorious whole on page 208). However, a three-dimensional spiral would be more accurate—a reminder that though we observe the same seasons year after year, God invites us to experience them afresh, drawing us ever upward to himself.

As we participate in the Cycle of Grace and the annual discipline of *remembering*, we join with the Holy Spirit in making the historical actions and the future promises of God present realities that they may shape us and our world. In Joshua 4:1-7, God tells Joshua to draw up twelve stones from the Jordan River and place them as a memorial:

> When your children ask in time to come, "What do those stones mean to you?" then you shall tell them that the waters of the Jordan were cut off before the ark of the covenant of the LORD.... So these stones shall be to the people of Israel a memorial forever (Joshua 4:6-7).

For the past 2,000 years, the seasons of the liturgical year have functioned as the remembrance stones of the church—they are the story of how Jesus, the new and better covenant, went before us, cutting off the mighty torrent of sin and death, allowing us to pass freely into the final promised land, the kingdom of heaven.

Let us respond to God's grace by being a people shaped, year after year, week after week, day after day, by the gospel story. Let us keep sacred time.

Call your people to remember you always.
O peoples of God! Remember your God!
    Remember him in all places.
    Remember him at all times.
    Remember his grace and his love.
    Remember his comfort and his mercy.
    Remember his beauty and his wonder.
    Remember his instruction and his holiness.
He is here. He is with you in every moment.

Every moment is holy.

Amen.

DOUGLAS MCKELVEY,
"A LITURGY FOR THE WRITING OF LITURGIES"

CYCLE OF LIGHT
GOD WITH US

Take your sandals off your feet, for the place on which you are standing is holy ground.
I am the God of your father, the God of Abraham, the God of Isaac, and the God of Jacob.
I have surely seen the affliction of my people.
I have heard their cry.
I know their sufferings, and I have come down to deliver them.

EXCERPTS FROM EXODUS 3:5-9

ADVENT

Ring out, wild bells, to the wild sky,
The flying cloud, the frosty light:
The year is dying in the night;
Ring out, wild bells, and let him die.

Ring out the old, ring in the new,
Ring, happy bells, across the snow:
The year is going, let him go;
Ring out the false, ring in the true.

Ring out the grief that saps the mind
For those that here we see no more;
Ring out the feud of rich and poor,
Ring in redress to all mankind.

Ring out a slowly dying cause,
And ancient forms of party strife;
Ring in the nobler modes of life,
With sweeter manners, purer laws.

Ring out the want, the care, the sin,
The faithless coldness of the times;
Ring out, ring out my mournful rhymes
But ring the fuller minstrel in.

Ring out false pride in place and blood,
The civic slander and the spite;
Ring in the love of truth and right,
Ring in the common love of good.

Ring out old shapes of foul disease;
Ring out the narrowing lust of gold;
Ring out the thousand wars of old,
Ring in the thousand years of peace.

Ring in the valiant man and free,
The larger heart, the kindlier hand;
Ring out the darkness of the land,
Ring in the Christ that is to be.

ALFRED LORD TENNYSON, "RING OUT, WILD BELLS"

STARTS: Four Sundays before Christmas
(between November 27 and December 3)

ENDS: December 24

TYPE: Preparation

DISCIPLINE: Silence

NOTABLE DATES:
Saint Nicholas
Saint Lucy
Gaudete Sunday
Christmas Eve

KEY VERSE: "In the wilderness prepare the way of the LORD;
make straight in the desert a highway for our God" (Isaiah 40:3).

HYMN: "O Come, O Come, Emmanuel"

FRUIT OF THE SPIRIT: Patience

While the days and weeks of Advent traditionally close out our calendar year, they are, in fact, the very beginning of the liturgical year. The first Sunday of Advent is the church's New Year's Day. Advent is also the preparatory period of the Cycle of Light. At the heart of this cycle we focus on God with us in the three comings of Christ: Jesus's arrival in historic time as Mary's son, Jesus's promised return at the end of time, and Jesus's entrance into our own lives.

Just as Sunday is both the first and eighth day of creation, Advent is both the first and the last season of the church year: the remembrance of the beginning of all things and an acknowledgment of the end of them. It rings in our ears like the first and eighth notes of the octave—the incarnation consonant with eschaton, our anticipation of the second coming producing a profound resonance with and greater revelation than the first.

History

The origins of the season of Advent are a bit murky. As the rhythms of the liturgical year were developed over several centuries, the season of Advent looked and functioned differently in various times and places. It seems the earliest record of a formal Advent-like season was observed during the three weeks preceding Epiphany (January 6), and these weeks were utilized as an intentional time of preparation for those wishing to be baptized on that day. Around AD 480, Perpetuus, bishop of Tours, shifted the celebratory emphasis from Epiphany to Christmas, and in the late sixth century, Pope Gregory I (Gregory the Great) fixed the season at four weeks.

Initially, Advent was a penitential season similar to Lent, but by the time the twelfth century rolled around, most of the penitential aspects of the season had been set aside

in favor of a more hope-filled, anticipatory posture. Unfortunately, in the past century, Advent has become synonymous with being a mere extension of the December 25 festivities. In the weeks preceding Christmas, we are expected to participate in the cultural hysteria of shopping, movie bingeing, light displays, extreme baking, holiday parties, and—don't forget!—shopping. But for the Christian, the true nature of Advent is somber, and traditional practices emphasize reflective waiting, quiet patience, and spiritual preparation.

Advent Places Us in God's Story

The term *Advent* is derived from the Latin *adventus*, meaning "coming," and possesses a dual meaning for the church. In Advent, we anticipate both the incarnation and Christ's return.

As the church calendar is intended to reflect the arc of redemption from creation to the second coming, the season of Advent represents thousands of years of God's work among his people, holding the entire weight of the Old Testament in its gentle four-week span. Advent invites us to remember how *very long* humanity waited for our Messiah.

But this season of reflection is also a reminder that in our present day and age, we are *still* Before Christ, perpetually inhabiting a second Advent. We still need our Savior to come and make all things new. Advent is a space to remember that longing for the Messiah isn't just a nice thing we say we do. It's the correct response to the genuine horror we should feel when we observe the devasting effects of sin in the world. As the people of God, sometimes we can best bear witness to the light by acknowledging the existence of the darkness.

For churches that follow the prescribed Scripture readings of the lectionary,[1] the lessons for the first Sunday in Advent have nothing to do with messianic prophecy and angelic pronouncements. Instead, the assigned readings are focused on the eschaton as an exhortation to the church to be ready and watchful. As the weeks progress toward Christmas, this theme continues, drawing on the ministry of John the Baptist and his fervent call to "repent, for the kingdom of heaven is at hand" (Matthew 3:2). The message of these readings is an exhortation for the faithful to take up John's cry in all seasons because "that day and hour no one knows" (Matthew 24:36).

The kingdom of heaven is coming in full. The question Advent probes in us is, Are we ready? Do we live as ones prepared for Jesus's promised return?

HOLY HUES

The liturgical color of Advent is violet (shifting to rose on Gaudete Sunday), though blue has also been used. (Blue is traditionally the color of hope and is also associated with Mary, the mother of Jesus.) While the use of violet in church is often a symbol of sorrow and penitence, it has a double meaning during Advent, signifying hopefulness as we look for the majesty and power of our coming King.

Advent Is a Spiritual Discipline

For humans who are hardwired to be tribal, few tasks are more challenging than being countercultural. It is extremely difficult to extricate yourself and your family from the Christmas mania happening during Advent. But the sacred rhythms of the church invite us to step away from the hysteria and into a holy wilderness.

Wilderness seasons are significant in the life of God's people. The Israelites wandered in the desert for forty years before entering the Promised Land. God was silent for 400 years before the birth of Christ. Jesus fasted in the desert for forty days before beginning his ministry. Sometimes we experience wilderness seasons too. Seasons of waiting and seasons of wandering are often uncomfortable, but God uses them to accomplish subtle work in our hearts, building muscles of discipline, patience, and faithfulness, readying us for what's to come. If we allow it, Advent can be a season oriented toward this kind of fruitfulness.

Consistently practicing the spiritual discipline of silence can be a great way to make space for prayerful wandering and intentional listening in an otherwise noisy life. Jesus proclaims, "He who has ears to hear, let him hear" (Mark 4:9). But it's hard to listen well when the world around us is *loud*. Jesus practiced solitude and silence with remarkable regularity, often withdrawing to be alone and pray (Luke 5:16). We should likewise be responsive to the needs of our souls. Our times of silence act as a mini-wilderness, allowing us to be open to God in a space beyond words. What a glorious way to enter into a holy Advent, making our hearts ready for Emmanuel, God with us.

> God far exceeds all words that we can here express.
> In silence He is heard, in silence worshipped best.[2]
>
> Angelus Silesius (1624–1677)

TIPS FOR PRACTICING SILENCE

- Go someplace quiet where you are unlikely to be interrupted. Silence your phone. Turn off any distractions (TV, music, annoying fan). Settle yourself comfortably but not in a posture of sleep.

- Start small—two to five minutes. Set a timer. Work your way up to ten or more minutes.

- Light a candle—flames have long represented the Holy Spirit. Focusing on the flame instead of closing your eyes can help keep your mind on the Lord.

- Begin by offering yourself to the Lord with the words of Isaiah, "Here I am," or Samuel, "Speak, Lord, your servant is listening." If you have something for which you are particularly seeking the Lord's counsel, ask him now.

- If your mind wanders, notice the wandering, gently release your thoughts to the Lord, and bring your attention back to God. Don't fret, you're only human. If you'd like, choose a Scripture to focus on and return to in these moments.

- Close your time by expressing to the Lord how the period of silence made you feel (uncomfortable? peaceful? indifferent? fidgety?), and thank the Lord for his sure presence (Zephaniah 3:17).

- Try to practice silence regularly—daily for a season, if you're able!—to train your head, heart, and hands in the practice of settling yourself before the Lord. The first few times are bound to be funky, especially if silence is something new to you or if your life is particularly full, noisy, or unsettled.

TIPS FOR PRACTICING SILENCE WITH CHILDREN

- Silence is a challenging discipline for many adults and will be that much more so for children, depending on their age.

- Preface your time of silence by reading the story of Elijah found in 1 Kings 19. Ask your kids a few probing questions, such as "Where did Elijah go to talk to God?" or "What happened when God finally spoke?"

- Tell your children you're all going to listen for God's voice for one minute. Remind them that listening means open ears and a quiet mouth. Set a timer that they can see. Tell them to get comfortable—to lie down, sit, or position themselves in a way that helps them feel calm.

- Start your timer and go. Don't be surprised if the first time (or ten) is a loud affair. This is a discipline, and building the muscles to do it well takes time. If one minute is too long, bump it down to thirty seconds. If you think your kids can do longer, add time in thirty-second increments.

- Afterward, offer a prayer of praise and thanksgiving.

ALTERNATIVELY...

- Think of a task you often do while listening to podcasts, music, or TV (like working out or driving), and instead, do it in silence. Just practice being present with the Lord in that activity.

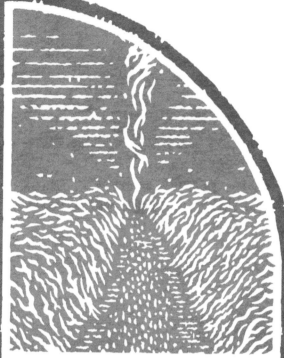

Advent Is Communal

While Advent is a time in which Christians can live especially counterculturally, please note that I am not advocating ignoring Christmas lights, rejecting Christmas cards or cookies, or acting like the Grinch.

If your communal gathering places (church, school, stores, etc.) are in full-on Christmas mode after Thanksgiving, it is still possible to have a quiet, reflective Advent with your family. Make your home a haven from the holiday hysteria. Set expectations with your children ahead of the first Sunday of Advent about how you intend to observe the pre-Christmas season.

Remember: Christmas starts on December 25 and lasts for twelve full days. You will get to do plenty of celebrating. There is no need for you and your family to experience holiday burnout before you make it to the feast season!

The family activities below are intended to be suggestions. Consider which traditions will invite your family into a rhythm of grace in this season. What will slow your hearts? What will orient your lives to the coming Lord? Ask yourself these questions each year—one year will look different from another as your family's priorities, schedules, ages, and life circumstances change.

Before Advent Begins

- Do all your Christmas shopping. Seriously. All of it. All the gifts for family and whoever else you may buy for. Finish before the first Sunday of Advent so it's not taking up space in your head during Advent. You won't regret it.

- Let every house prepare him room! Clean out your stuff. Go through your kids' possessions *with* your kids, pick items that can be donated ahead of Christmas, and donate them. The adults in the family should go through their own belongings too. Use the time to pray about what the Lord has for you this season.

Sundays During Advent

Advent starts four Sundays before Christmas and ends on Christmas Eve. Use each Sunday in Advent as an opportunity to slowly develop your favorite traditions.

Christmas Tree

The Christmas tree is, perhaps, the most popular and beloved symbol of Christmas in the world. Its evergreen boughs—so steadfast that even winter cannot kill them—are icons of Christ's love and our everlasting life in him; the lights on the tree are reminders of Christ's light to the world. While a wonderful part of our holiday traditions, the tree is a *Christmas* tree, not an Advent tree. There's no need to rush to get the tree up the day after Thanksgiving (or rush to take it down December 26). Take the full four weeks to fully decorate your tree:

- First Sunday: Put up the bare tree.
- Second Sunday: Light the tree (or you can wait to light it until the Feast of Saint Lucy, December 13, which is usually close to the second Sunday of Advent—see page 51 to learn more).
- Third Sunday: Add half your ornaments.
- Fourth Sunday: Finish placing the ornaments.
- Christmas Eve: Top your tree.

Don't put any gifts under the tree until Christmas morning. Or...don't even decorate your tree until Christmas Eve. Remember, the tree stays up until Epiphany (or Candlemas on February 2, if you're hard-core—see page 87). You'll have time to enjoy it!

Nativity

Saint Francis of Assisi created the first nativity display in AD 1223, and the personal nativity set became popular in the eighteenth century. It is a wonderful way to bring the Christmas story alive in your home. If you have a set, release the pieces slowly—a few each Sunday in Advent.

- First Sunday: Put up the creche (or stable).
- Second Sunday: Add the sheep and shepherds in the fields.
- Third Sunday: Place the barnyard animals in the stable (and the empty manger if baby Jesus is removable).
- Fourth Sunday: Add Mary and Joseph.
- Christmas Eve: Put Jesus in the manger.

Remember, the wise men and camels don't arrive until January 5! It's traditional to keep your nativity set up through Candlemas on February 2.

Advent Wreath

Advent wreaths are of German origin and officially date back to the sixteenth century. The original practice of the Advent wreath was simply focused on the coming light of Christ. The idea is that each week, we add a little more light to our homes and hearts, building anticipation for Jesus's birth. The wreath makes a wonderful centerpiece for your dining table, and lighting the candles can be a special part of your family's tradition each Sunday—perhaps a time to pray or reflect together on Advent. Notice how much brighter your home gets each week as you keep watch for the inbreaking Light of the World.

There are a number of ways to assemble and light your wreath. Traditionally, Advent wreaths consist of four candles: three violet candles and a rose candle. One candle is lit each Sunday in Advent, saving the rose candle for Gaudete Sunday on the third week (page 52). All white candles can also be used. There is an "expanded" version of the tradition that includes a fifth candle (a white one, also called the Christ candle), which is lit on Christmas Eve.

Devotional Practices

Advent Calendars

This name is a bit of a misnomer as "Advent" calendars almost universally begin on December 1, whereas Advent can begin in November or as late as December 3. Regardless, these calendars are a wonderful way to count down to Christmas, especially with children. The standard Advent calendar has one special door (or pouch) to open for each day in December and often contains a chocolate or some other type of toy or treat. You can buy these premade (and pre-stuffed) or create your own!

Jesse Tree

The Jesse Tree is an especially meaningful Advent calendar that takes the reader on a journey through the story of Scripture from creation to the incarnation. Each day there is a symbol and an assigned reading. This tradition reminds us how long Israel waited for the Messiah and how God works in unusual people and unexpected ways. Generally, this activity includes some way of displaying the day's symbol so that you can see the symbols accumulate over Advent and easily review the story. If you choose to keep your tree bare of ornaments until Christmas Eve, adding one Jesse Tree ornament per day can be a great way of watching the story unfold over four weeks.

Listen to Advent Hymns

Did you know Advent hymns are different from Christmas carols? While it is impossible to fully escape the carols during Advent, definitely be intentional about singing Advent hymns with your family. These hymns often draw out the themes of preparation, readiness, and longing. Here are a few favorites:

"Come, Thou Long Expected Jesus"

"Let All Mortal Flesh Keep Silence"

"Lo, He Comes with Clouds Descending"

"O Come, O Come, Emmanuel"

"Lo, How a Rose E'er Blooming"

Practice Silence as a Family

Perhaps when you light your Advent candle each week, take a few minutes for reflective silence. Remind each other that the people of God waited a long time for Jesus and that we are still waiting for him to return. Quietly wait for him together for a few minutes. Talk about what was hard about the waiting—and perhaps enjoy a treat afterward, a reminder that good things come to those who wait!

Fast

While fasting is no longer a communal tradition during Advent, it can still be a beneficial practice for experiencing an immediate and present longing, thereby increasing anticipation of Christmas Day. Fasting as a discipline will be dealt with more fully in the Lent chapter (pages 111-117).

Fasting doesn't necessarily mean abstaining from all food. It may be beneficial to simply abstain from indulgences—desserts or adult beverages, for instance. You could even fast from non-consumables like electronics (podcasts, music, TV) as a means of practicing silence, or from electric light to foster an appreciation of the coming light of Christ. Note that Christians *never* fast on Sundays, and it is acceptable to break fasts for special feast days (like the Feast of Saint Nicholas or Saint Lucy in Advent).

One other option is to prepare simplified meals for the duration of Advent (excepting Sundays)—soups, salads, sandwiches, Crock-Pot dishes, and plainer fare that does not require a lot of preparation or cooking. Save your fancy meals for Sundays and Christmastide!

No-Knead Bread

Making bread that requires a rise is a wonderful way to develop the themes of waiting with your kids. This no-knead bread is simple and easy (great to do with kids) but requires at least a five-hour rise. An overnight rise works great for this recipe, but if you're using this as a teachable moment about waiting, daytime is best so you can check on it together to see how the dough grows.

This recipe has been a family favorite in my house since the first time I made it for my husband as a newlywed. For years it was the recipe I used to bake bread for my church to serve at Communion. It is cooked in a Dutch oven, so the outside gets nice and crisp. It's best on the first day, but it does make yummy toast on days two and three.

Before you begin, read Luke 13:20-21 together: Jesus said, "What else is the Kingdom of God like? It is like the yeast a woman used in making bread. Even though she put only a little yeast in three measures of flour, it permeated every part of the dough" (NLT). As you watch your dough rise, point out how such a small amount of yeast makes such a big difference in your bread.

Servings: 10

INGREDIENTS

3 cups all-purpose flour
1¾ tsp. salt
½ tsp. active dry yeast
1½ cups water, room temperature

DIRECTIONS

1. In a big bowl, mix the flour, salt, and yeast. Pour the water into the bowl and use a spatula or a wooden spoon to mix it until well incorporated. You do not need to activate the yeast before adding it to the flour; the slow rising process will do the trick.

2. Cover the bowl with plastic wrap and let it sit on your counter or inside your unheated oven for at least 5 hours, or up to 24 hours. The dough should double in size and be full of air holes.

3. When you're ready to bake, preheat the oven to 450°F. Add your Dutch oven (with the lid on) to the oven as it's preheating so the pot becomes nice and hot for baking. When the oven is fully preheated, remove the pot from the oven and remove the lid.

4. Sprinkle flour on your hands, over the dough, and directly into the bottom of the pot. With your floured hands, gently remove the dough from the bowl, and roughly shape it into a ball. Take the ball of dough and drop it gently into the pot. Cover the pot with the lid and place it back in the oven. Alternatively, you can place the ball of dough on a piece of parchment paper, then lift the parchment paper by the corners and drop both it and the dough into the pot. This will also ensure that your bread doesn't stick at all to the bottom of the pot. If you use parchment paper, the bread doesn't brown as much on the sides, but otherwise it's still crusty and delicious.

5. Bake for 30 minutes with the lid on, then remove the lid and bake for another 15 to 20 minutes, or until golden brown. Remove the bread from the pot; it should fall out easily. Let it cool completely before slicing and serving.

Adapted with gratitude from Jo Cooks.

Liturgical Practices
Saint Nicholas Day—December 6

Nicholas was born in the late third century to wealthy parents in what is now southwestern Turkey. He joined a monastery at the age of seventeen and, while still a young man, was chosen to be the archbishop of Myra. As archbishop, he was present at the Council of Nicaea in AD 325 and helped draft the Nicene Creed, which is still recited in thousands of churches across the globe each Sunday.

Nick is most famous for having lived in a posture of openhanded generosity, so much so that the stories of his charity inspired the legends of Santa Claus! In one such story, Nicholas learned of a ruined family who couldn't provide dowries for their daughters. Wanting to help but not wanting to be identified as the helper, he threw gold coins down their chimney. Some of these landed in the family's socks, which were hanging in the hearth to dry. From this story we get the tradition of Christmas stockings and Saint Nicholas Day shoes.

Because of his virtue, Nick was admired throughout Asia Minor. The day of his death—December 6—was declared a feast day, a celebration of Christ's work in the life of Nicholas, and a day on which gifts were given in honor of the charity he displayed.

Celebrating Saint Nicholas

Traditionally, on the eve of December 6, families leave out a snack for Saint Nicholas, a carrot for his donkey, and empty shoes. In the morning, the food is gone, and the shoes are filled with treats and toys. (You can see the original contours of the Santa Claus legends in the tradition as over time, this morphed into reindeer, milk, and cookies.) Chocolate coins wrapped in gold foil and oranges (alluding to the round, gold coins) are common Saint Nicholas Day shoe-fillers.

If you're looking for an additional teaching moment, recite the Nicene Creed together, and thank God for the faithful men and women of previous generations who worked so hard to protect and preserve the church.

BUT WHAT ABOUT SANTA?

In our current cultural moment, it is impossible to get through the Advent season without a reminder of Santa on every street corner (often quite literally). Whether or not you incorporate Santa Claus into your December 25 traditions is a matter of Christian prudence. But for those who find that "Santa" takes up a little too much space in your children's hearts on Christmas Day, the Feast of Saint Nicholas may be a perfect way to incorporate "Santa" in the season, but reserve December 25 for Jesus. When Saint Nicholas "comes" on December 6, use it as an opportunity to talk about the historic Nicholas who wanted nothing more than to point people to God with his gift giving. Allow December 6 to become a small taste of Christmas, a reminder that *all gifts* point us to God's greatest gift, Jesus!

Saint Lucy's Day—December 13

Lucy was a devout young woman living in Italy in the third century, and she is, perhaps, most famous for her (totally fictional) role in Dante's *Divine Comedy* and her legendary appearance on Lake Vänern in a boat full of wheat on the darkest night of the year, which saved the Swedish people from famine. As a young woman, Lucy never married, choosing instead to dedicate her life to the church and give all her money to the poor. She was martyred by Roman soldiers for her faith at twenty-one years old. On December 13, Lucy is remembered for her innocence, devotion to God, courage, and service to the church.

Celebrating Saint Lucy

Lucy means "light," and as such, her feast day is particularly appropriate for the Advent season. On the old calendar, the winter solstice—the longest night of the year—was on December 13, and, especially in Scandinavia, Saint Lucy's Day is also known as the Festival of Light. Her feast is a perfect day for lighting your Christmas tree or the outside of your home.

Traditionally on Saint Lucy's Day, the oldest daughter in the family wakes early, dons a Saint Lucy costume, and serves Saint Lucy's buns (also known as saffron buns, *lussekatter*, and Saint Lucia buns) to the rest of her family in their beds. Saint Lucia buns are shaped to look like a pair of eyes, as Lucy is the patron saint of the blind. If serving homemade *lussekatter* in bed is out of the realm of possibility for your family in this season, enjoy some store-bought cinnamon rolls around the dining table, and perhaps allow your oldest girl to serve them! Feel free to defer the celebration to the nearest weekend.

Gaudete Sunday

This is the third Sunday of Advent and takes its name from the Latin *gaudete*, meaning "rejoice!" The opening reading for this Sunday is taken from Philippians 4:4: "Rejoice in the Lord always; again I will say, rejoice." The liturgical color shifts from violet to rose on this day, representing a lightening of the darkness. Remember to light your rose-colored candle today. On Gaudete Sunday, the lectionary readings shift from the eschaton to the testimony of John the Baptist and the imminence of Christ's coming. The good news of great joy is almost here!

Stir-Up Sunday

The prayer for the fourth Sunday of Advent begins, "Stir up your power, O Lord, and with great might come among us." It's a prayer for endurance as we wait for Jesus! "Stir-Up Sunday" is a charming British custom wherein the prayer served as a reminder for families to "stir up" their Christmas pudding so it would have adequate time to "cure" on the counter and be ready to serve on Christmas. (Christmas pudding[3] is a traditional English dessert that contained thirteen ingredients—twelve for the apostles and one for Christ. Each member of the family would take turns stirring the thick pudding, and they stirred from east to west to remember the journey of the wise men to Christ.) If you want to do a Christmas pudding, mix it up on the fourth Sunday of Advent and serve it on the final day of Christmas (January 5) as a king cake (more on that in the next chapter) so it has sufficient time to age. If Christmas pudding isn't your thing, the fourth Sunday of Advent is a great day for baking! Bake Christmas treats for neighbors, church leaders, friends, and colleagues. The next recipes are two of my family's favorite treats to enjoy during Christmastide.

JEN'S HOT BUTTERED RUM

This is one of my family's Christmas delights and perfect for sipping on Christmas Eve.
For the children or those who don't imbibe, a rumless "Hot Buttered" is also delicious!

Servings: 16

INGREDIENTS

½ cup butter, softened
½ cup plus 2 T. brown sugar
¾ cup plus 1 T. powdered sugar
1 pint French vanilla ice cream, melted
1 tsp. vanilla
1 tsp. cinnamon
1 tsp. nutmeg
Spiced brown rum (optional)

DIRECTIONS

1. Soften the ice cream in a bowl until it reaches a pourable consistency.

2. Soften the butter to room temperature in another bowl, then beat in the brown and powdered sugars until light and fluffy. Stir in the ice cream until well blended.

3. Stir in the vanilla, cinnamon, and nutmeg.

4. Store the drink in the fridge for 5 to 7 days or freeze for up to 6 months.

TO SERVE

Add 3 tablespoons of the cream mixture and 3 tablespoons of rum to a mug. Fill the rest of the mug with hot water and stir. Garnish with a cinnamon stick and lemon twist if desired.

MOM'S CHERRY ALMOND BISCOTTI

Biscotti are wonderful anytime, but they are especially delicious with your
favorite seasonal drink in front of the warm glow of the Christmas tree.
Also, 1:1 gluten-free flour works great in this recipe if you're gluten intolerant.

Yield: 25 biscotti

INGREDIENTS

- ¼ cup light extra-virgin olive oil
- ¼ cup unsalted butter, melted
- 1 cup granulated sugar
- 2 tsp. almond extract
- 1 tsp. vanilla extract
- 3 large eggs
- 2½ cups all-purpose flour (or Bob's Red Mill Gluten-Free 1:1 Baking Flour)
- ½ cup almond meal
- ¼ tsp. salt
- 1 T. baking powder
- 1 cup dried cherries, finely chopped

DIRECTIONS

1. Preheat the oven to 375°F. Line a large baking sheet with parchment paper. Set aside.

2. In a medium bowl, cream together the oil, butter, and sugar. Beat in the almond and vanilla extracts, followed by the eggs.

3. In a separate bowl, combine the flour, almond meal, salt, and baking powder. Slowly add the flour mixture to the egg mixture. Mix just until a smooth dough forms. Stir in the cherries.

4. Shape the dough into two 12 x 2-inch logs that are about ½ inch thick, and place them on the prepared baking sheet.

5. Bake for 25 to 30 minutes or until lightly golden brown. Keep the oven on as you allow the logs to cool enough to touch. Cut 1-inch diagonal slices. Lay each slice cut side down on the baking sheet and return it to the oven for another 10 minutes or until lightly toasted on each side. Cool completely on a wire rack. Store in an airtight container at room temperature for up to 2 weeks or in the freezer for up to 3 months.

Christmas Eve

For many, church on Christmas Eve is the tradition that kicks off the Christmas festivities. This practice can be traced back to the Jewish tradition of beginning a feast the "night before," as Jews believed that a day began in the evening. The church likewise adapted this tradition for many of its major feasts, and so commenced the Feast of the Nativity of Our Lord Jesus Christ the evening of December 24. Originally this looked like a midnight church service. To accommodate families, this was gradually moved back to an earlier time in the evening. Whatever time you celebrate, go to a Christmas Eve service and enjoy the lovely candlelit worship, hear the news of the angelic proclamation, and sing along with them, "Glory to God in the highest, and on earth peace, and good will to men!" (Luke 2:14 KJV).

LITURGY FOR ADVENT

Before you begin, light a candle (or the appropriate candles on your Advent wreath) and open your Bible to the week's reading. If you plan to observe a time of silence, also have your timer handy. The words in **bold** are intended for everyone to say together as they are able.

Opening

"In the wilderness prepare the way of the LORD; make straight in the desert a highway for our God" (Isaiah 40:3).

Antiphon

On December 17 through 23, replace this antiphon with the appropriate O Antiphon for that day (see page 57).

Our King and Savior now draws near:

O come, let us adore him.

Psalm 126

Scripture Reading

Anyone may do the reading. Once the reading has finished, perhaps take a minute to discuss and reflect on it together.

First week of Advent—Mark 13:24-37

Second week of Advent—Isaiah 11:1-10

Third week of Advent—John 1:19-29

Fourth week of Advent—Luke 1:26-38

Silence

If you'd like, take this time to sit quietly with the Lord and silently reflect on the reading. Set a timer for two to five minutes (or less, if you're doing this with children).

Sing Together

"O Come, O Come, Emmanuel"

Pray

Take this time to pray as a family, lifting up your own needs and the needs of your community.

Lord's Prayer

Closing Prayer

Hasten, O Father, the coming of your kingdom; and grant that we your servants, who now live by faith, may with joy behold your Son at his coming in glorious majesty; even Jesus Christ, our only Mediator and Advocate. Amen.[4]

O Antiphons

Each of these seven ancient prayers begins with the word "O," followed by a prophetic name for the Messiah and the supplication "Come." The names are often recognized as the inspiration for the text of "O Come, O Come, Emmanuel."

December 17: O WISDOM, you came forth from the mouth of the Most High, and reaching from beginning to end, you ordered all things mightily and sweetly.

Come and teach us the way of prudence!

December 18: O LORD AND RULER (Adonai) of the House of Israel, who appeared to Moses in the flame of the burning bush and gave him the law on Sinai:

Come, and redeem us with outstretched arms.

December 19: O ROOT OF JESSE, who stands for a sign among the people, before whom the kings keep silence and unto whom the nations make their prayer:

Come, deliver us, and tarry not.

December 20: O KEY OF DAVID, and scepter of the House of Israel, who opens and no one shuts, who shuts and no one opens:

Come, and bring forth the captive from his prison, he who sits in darkness and in the shadow of death.

December 21: O DAWN OF THE EAST, brightness of light eternal and sun of justice:

Come, and enlighten those who sit in darkness and in the shadow of death.

December 22: O KING OF THE NATIONS and their desire, the cornerstone that makes both one:

Come, and deliver us, whom you formed out of the dust of the earth.

December 23: O EMMANUEL, God with us, our king and lawgiver, the expected of the nations and their Savior:

Come to save us, O Lord our God.

CHRISTMAS

It was a time like this,
War & tumult of war,
a horror in the air.
Hungry yawned the abyss—
and yet there came the star
and the child most wonderfully there.

It was a time like this
of fear & lust for power,
license & greed and blight—
and yet the Prince of bliss
came into the darkest hour
in quiet & silent light.

And in a time like this
how celebrate his birth
when all things fall apart?
Ah! wonderful it is
with no room on the earth
the stable is our heart.

Madeleine L'Engle
"Into the Darkests Hour"

STARTS: December 25

ENDS: January 5

TYPE: Celebration

DISCIPLINE: Feasting

NOTABLE DATES:
The Nativity of Our Lord
Saint Stephen
Saint John
The Holy Innocents
The Holy Name of Jesus
The Holy Family

KEY VERSE: "The Word became flesh and dwelt among us, and we have seen his glory" (John 1:14).

HYMN: "Joy to the World"

FRUIT OF THE SPIRIT: Peace

Celebrated in 160 countries, Christmas hardly needs an introduction. But did you know this holiday isn't just one day but an entire season? December 25 merely *commences* the twelve days of Christmas—also known as Christmastide—a season of celebrating the good news of great joy that is for all people!

History

Christmas was originally known as the Feast of the Nativity of Our Lord Jesus Christ. The church service in honor of this feast was colloquially referred to as "Christ's Mass," which was eventually shortened to "Christmas" in the eleventh century.

The earliest records of a formally observed Christmas date to AD 336. It appears that at this time, the date of Jesus's birth was being used by Roman Christians as a reason to participate in the festivities of Saturnalia. Thus the season of Christmastide began organically taking shape. While December 25 was not celebrated as Christ's birth *for* this reason, the concurrence of Christ's Nativity with Saturnalia made it easy for many of the traditions of the pagan feast to become Christian customs (with a religious spin added, of course!):

- Gift giving—we celebrate that Jesus is God's greatest gift to us.

- Role reversal—we celebrate that the Creator of heaven and earth humbled himself and took on infant flesh.

- Games and parties—we celebrate with delight and feasting as a symbol of the coming wedding feast of the lamb, a fitting culmination of the Advent season of longing.

As the years went on and Christmas celebrations grew and spread, the customs of the season continued to be adapted based on local midwinter rituals. Modern-day Christmases reflect the numerous co-opted multicultural traditions.

Christians today hold in tension the actual nativity of Christ with the pagan roots of certain celebratory traditions. While many of the pleasures of the Christmas season do not originate explicitly in Scripture or from church history and tradition, we can still choose to enjoy these good, beautiful, and true things in honor of the author of all that is good, true, and beautiful. Let us walk prudently in the steps of the saints who have come before, enjoying the many wonderful things God's good world has to offer as we celebrate the gift of Christ, the baby born to die that we might be welcomed into God's glorious, upside-down kingdom.

WAS JESUS REALLY BORN ON DECEMBER 25?

The method by which December 25 was determined to be Christ's birth by some of the early Christian writers is varied and in some cases unclear, but for Irenaeus (AD 120-202) and Julius Africanus (AD 221), the date of Christ's birth seems to have been determined by the historical context of John the Baptist's conception.

Scholars believe Zechariah was serving in the temple on the Day of Atonement (generally in September) when the angel appeared to reveal John's conception (Luke 1:3-11). John's birth is traditionally celebrated on June 24 (roughly nine months after his conception).

Scripture tells us that the angel appears to Mary approximately six months into Elizabeth's pregnancy (Luke 1:26), which would be late March. This dating puts Jesus's birth in late December. While there is no way of knowing for sure that Jesus was born on December 25, it's a relatively reasonable bet that he was at least born *around* that date.

Christmas Places Us in God's Story

While the focus of Advent is on our past and present experience of *chronos* as we wait and long for the coming Messiah, the season of Christmas is a celebration of *kairos*—the opportune moment in which God entered history, time, and our very own lives. Christmas is the answered prayer of a desperate people: How long, O Lord? (Psalm 13:1). It is the hope for an answer to our own fervent prayer: Come, Lord Jesus (Revelation 22:20). In the story of God, Christmas—the incarnation—is the point at which each of our lives finds its start, "the beginning of our never-ending gladness."[1] There is no Christian without there first having been Christ.

The doctrine of the incarnation lies at the heart of the Christmas celebration—a season for standing in open-mouthed awe at the "great exchange" when eternity irrevocably merges with time, the eternally begotten one is born, the author of all life is subjected to death, *the very Word of God becomes flesh and dwells among us*. Christmas is about the moment God loved humanity so much that he permanently became like us so we could become like him.

In our remembering of Christmastide, we make present Christ's coming once again as we wonder at his entrance into our lives and the world, and at the global transformation promised at his birth. We rightly respond: "Glory to God in the highest, and on earth peace, good will toward men" (Luke 2:14 KJV).

Christmas Is a Spiritual Discipline

A life lived in overindulgence will likely yield ugly fruit, but two seasons of the church year call for no-holds-barred celebration: Christmas and Easter. And these feasts last for an entire *season*—not just December 25 and Easter Sunday but the weeks that follow (Christmastide and Eastertide).

> "On this mountain the LORD of hosts will make for all people a feast of rich food, a feast of well-aged wine, of rich food full of marrow, of aged wine well refined." ISAIAH 25:6

Jesus is a fan of the feast. In his first miracle, he turned water into wine so a wedding celebration could continue. Later, he participated in the Passover feast on the night he was arrested. And when all is said and done, we are invited to delight ourselves at the wedding feast of the Lamb—the banquet to end all banquets.

A good celebration is one that engages the participant in creation in such a way as to posture him or her in gratitude and worship to the Creator. As we feast, we imitate Christ and honor him, acknowledging the tremendous gravity of the incarnation (at Christmas) and the resurrection (at Easter). Feasting during Christmastide is simply obeying with utmost seriousness the angelic call: "Rejoice!"

> "Oh, taste and see that the LORD is good!" PSALM 34:8

While feasting seems like it would be an easy discipline to enter into, it can be harder than you might think. Sitting in abundance and rest when you're ready to move on is challenging! There will be years when you'll be tempted to end Christmastide feasting early (or skip it altogether) and get back to normal life. Honor the time the Lord has given you to celebrate, even when it feels incongruous with what you're walking through. Perhaps in a hard season, feasting will be the place where the Lord most unexpectedly meets you.

TIPS FOR FEASTING DURING CHRISTMASTIDE

For each family, feasting will look a bit different—especially depending on the ages of your kids—but here are a few suggestions:

- Let each person in the family set a dinner menu over the course of the twelve days of Christmas (dessert and a special drink included!) or go out to dinner or order in a couple times during the twelve days.

- Have a family movie night or go see a movie together.

- Take all twelve days off from paid work.

- Do something unusual and special as a family—go on a hiking trip, spend the day at an amusement park or indoor playground, build a big puzzle, or have a baking contest, Mario-Kart tournament, dance party, or living room campout.

- Host family and friends, especially on the twelfth night.

- Pray together each day, telling each other the story of God's work at Christmas and remembering (making alive!) the incarnation in your own hearts and home.

- Take extra time to enjoy your favorite activities (as individuals or families), and delight in the ways those things nurture gratitude for God and one another.

Christmas Is Communal

If you observe a traditional Advent, then your Christmastide will also be relatively countercultural. Luckily, it's far easier to convince people to join you in a season of feasting than it is to invite them into a season of wilderness. Christmastide is naturally a time when families and friends gather to celebrate (plus, if your community isn't keen on joining you in the feast season, more cookies for you!).

Before Christmastide

Decide which traditions you want to participate in and prepare accordingly. Plan for the twelve days of Christmas like prepping for a big party or hosting Thanksgiving. If you can, plan for Christmastide before Advent while you're getting your Christmas shopping done. Map out which days you're giving which gifts so you know what you want to purchase. While the preplanning can be challenging, you won't regret having the space during Advent to quiet your heart or the space during Christmas to enjoy the fruits of your efforts.

REMINDER

While many people like to use January 1 as a date for kicking off their New Year's resolutions—many of which call for greater self-control in areas of eating and exercise—I encourage you to push off starting these new routines until after January 6. Enjoy a full Christmastide of feasting without the constraints of the secular calendar.

Christmas Traditions

Each family has their own Christmas Day traditions—in general, keep these! They're an important part of your family's story. Keep in mind that observing Christmastide as a feast season gives us any number of excuses to practice hospitality and serve our non-Christian neighbors as well. Here's a quick overview of traditions, many of which offer opportunities to be countercultural in a non-grinchy way:

- **Go to church.** Most families go on Christmas Eve—after all, Christmas starts at nightfall on December 24. Worshipping on Christmas morning is also a lovely way to begin this festal season.
- **Give gifts.** Traditionally, gifts were given each of the twelve days of Christmas. Consider spreading your gifting out over twelve days. This has the benefit of allowing kids to really enjoy their gifts instead of simply moving on to open the next

thing. Activity gifts are perfect for the latter days of Christmastide, like a new board game or tickets to a special event or activity.

- **Send Christmas cards.** Just a friendly reminder that they are *Christmas* cards, not Advent cards. It's perfectly acceptable to send them between December 25 and January 6. Perhaps make the stuffing and addressing a family event as a part of your twelve days of celebration!

- **Bake cookies.** Post-Christmas is the best time for baking and giving cookies. Use this time to bake together as a family, then deliver the treats to your friends and neighbors.

- **Keep your Christmas tree up.** I cannot say this emphatically enough! It's a *Christmas* tree, not an Advent tree. The tree stays up until Christmastide is over (January 6).

- **Host a Christmas party.** Yes, Christmastide is the most appropriate time to have a *Christmas* party. Every year my family hosts a New Year's Day potluck brunch wherein we invite everyone we can reasonably fit in our home (and a dozen more besides). A horde of children destroy our playroom and people drop in as they're able, sharing food and conversation. We love starting our year with this kind of hospitality.

- **Sing Christmas carols.** 'Tis the season to blast the Christmas music 24/7. Play your favorite Christmas music, secular and sacred. You could even host a sing-along for friends and neighbors or go caroling!

- **Watch Christmas movies.** This is a fun and low-key family activity (perfect for day eight or nine of the feast when you're feeling ready to eat healthy food and get back to a regular schedule again).

Liturgical Traditions

Within the twelve days, there are five additional feasts following Christmas Day. The three days after December 25 are feasts in honor of the three types of martyrs of the church—those who are willing to die and are executed for their faith (Saint Stephen), those who are willing to die but are not executed (Saint John the Evangelist), those who are not willing to die but are still executed because of their association with Jesus (the young boys killed by Herod's decree, also known as the Holy Innocents). As we celebrate the birth of Jesus, we also celebrate the birth of these saints into the kingdom of heaven on the day of their deaths. While it may seem strange to spend the second, third, and fourth days of a celebratory feast remembering the sobering details of these saints' lives, it serves as a reminder of the ultimate purpose of Christ's birth: his death. It's a call to

CHRISTMAS CORNFLAKE WREATHS

In case your family needs any ideas of what to bake during Christmastide, try these! I've made these treats every Christmas since I can remember. Something about the combination of cornflakes and marshmallow is *so* delicious. My husband—who hates all dyed food—has insisted that we forego green food coloring in this recipe. Instead, we call these "snowy wreaths" and enjoy our marshmallows undyed, thank you very much. I also recommend using Kellogg's Corn Flakes over other brands, but to each their own!

Yield: 12 cookies

INGREDIENTS

1 stick (½ cup) butter
1 (10 oz.) bag large marshmallows
6 drops green gel food coloring or 1¼ tsp. green liquid food coloring (optional)
5 cups cornflakes
⅓ to ½ cup red-hot candies or red candy-coated chocolates such as mini M&M's
Cooking spray

DIRECTIONS

1. Line a sheet pan with parchment paper or a silicone baking mat.

2. Place the butter in a large stockpot over medium heat. When the butter is melted, rotate the pot to coat 2 to 3 inches up the sides.

3. Add the marshmallows to the pot, and stir as they melt, keeping the burner on medium heat. Continue stirring until the marshmallow is smooth.

4. Add the green food coloring (if using) to the marshmallow and stir to create a uniform color.

5. Turn off the heat and add the cornflakes slowly. Gently stir to coat the cereal evenly with the marshmallow mixture. Add more cornflakes if the marshmallow still seems to overwhelm the cornflakes.

6. To form each wreath, pack the mixture into a greased ½-cup measuring cup, then turn it out onto the sheet pan. Use your fingers to make a hole in the middle to form a wreath shape, then decorate the wreath with red candies. It's easiest to form the wreath holes if your fingers are damp or coated in cooking spray.

7. Cool completely (if you can wait that long) and serve.

remember that even as we find Christ born in us, we must deny ourselves, take up our cross, and follow him.

Feast of Saint Stephen—December 26

Stephen—"a man full of faith and of the Holy Spirit" (Acts 6:5)—was a deacon in the early church and the first martyr of the Christian faith. For his boldness in preaching the gospel, he was stoned by a frenzied pack of Jewish religious leaders. With his dying breath, Stephen prayed that God would forgive the sins of his killers. His example is a reminder to be a bold witness for the gospel and to forgive our enemies.

Celebrating Saint Stephen

Stephen's feast day is December 26, also known as Boxing Day. Originally, December 25 was reserved for worship services with a mass on Christmas Eve, Christmas morning, and Christmas afternoon. December 26 was therefore set aside for giving boxes (presents!). Later, as Christmas gifting moved to Christmas Day, Boxing Day became a day for giving gifts to the poor and your servants (if you had them).

Give

This day is perfect for giving gifts or treats to teachers, mail carriers, and other members of the community who regularly provide a service to your family.

Read

Acts 7 (or just 7:54-60 if you're short on time)

Sing Together

"Good King Wenceslas"

Pray

O Glorious Lord, your servant Stephen looked up to heaven and prayed for his persecutors: Grant that in all our sufferings here upon earth we may love and forgive our enemies, looking steadfastly to Jesus Christ our Lord, who sits at your right hand and intercedes for us; and who lives and reigns with you and the Holy Spirit, one God, now and for ever. **Amen.**[2]

Feast of Saint John—December 27

On the third day of Christmas, we celebrate Saint John the Evangelist (not "the Baptist"—his feast day is in June). This John is the apostle, brother of James, son of thunder, the disciple whom Jesus loved, and author of the Gospel of John, Revelation, and (probably) 1, 2, and 3 John. John was the only apostle at the foot of the cross as Jesus died, and the man to whom Jesus entrusted the care of his mother. He lived to be nearly one hundred and is the only one of the twelve apostles to have died of natural causes. This is not for lack of execution attempts on the part of the Romans—John is said to have survived drinking a cup of poisoned wine and being boiled alive in hot oil. For his apparent inability to be martyred, he was exiled to the Greek island of Patmos.

John's witness is a reminder of God's gracious deliverance and faithfulness. His loyalty to Jesus and deep identity as the beloved of God should serve as encouragement in our own walk with the Lord.

Celebrating Saint John

It is traditional on the Feast of Saint John to bless a bottle of wine. In the Bible, wine is a symbol of transformation and new life, of hospitality and abundance. And on this day, it's also a reminder of John's survived assassination attempt—the poisoned wine that did not kill him. In moderation, wine is a gift from the Lord, and blessing it is a way of marking it out for holy purpose—to facilitate welcome in your home and give thanks for God's good gifts.

BLESSING OVER WINE

Blessed are you, O Lord our God, who brings forth the fruit of vine: Grant that we who share this wine, which gladdens our hearts, may share forever the new life of the true vine, your Son Jesus Christ our Lord. Amen.

Adapted from the Book of Occasional Services[3]

If your pastor doesn't bless wine, you can also buy a bottle, bless it yourselves, and share it. If you don't drink alcohol, you could go an untraditional route and enjoy a fondue dinner in honor of John's unsuccessful boiling. Find a recipe for hot oil fondue and cook up some meat and veggies. Cheese or chocolate fondues are also delicious options (and loved by kids!).

Read
Mark 1:16-20; John 1:1-18

Pray
Shed upon your Church, O Lord, the brightness of your light; that we, being illumined by the teaching of your apostle, and evangelist John, may so walk in the light of your truth, that at length we may attain to the fullness of eternal life; through Jesus Christ our Lord, who lives and reigns with you and the Holy Spirit, one God, for ever and ever. **Amen.**[4]

On the fourth day of Christmas we turn our attention to the most painful and tragic of the martyrs—the little boys murdered at Herod's command. The church has traditionally remembered these precious little ones as the first martyrs for the faith.

The church has long struggled to determine how to appropriately bear witness to this tragedy. Ultimately, it was decided to use this day to remember God's love and care for little ones. We hold the tragedy and joy in tension with one another, rejoicing in the entrance of the boys into God's glorious kingdom, yet grieving for the families that lost their sons and brothers, and praising God for the gift of the children in our own lives.

Celebrating the Holy Innocents

As tradition goes, this was the day for the youngest to preside in the household, monastery or convent, or the church. Some even went so far as to only eat "baby" food for the day: soups, purees, oatmeal, and so forth. If that's not appealing—and let's face it, it's really not—Kendra Tierney at Catholic All Year puts a delicious twist on this tradition by preparing a big pot of cheese grits and a topping bar with food like shrimp, sausage, green onions, and corn. Crown your youngest king or queen for the day and make it a "yes!" day—whatever they ask (within reason), just say yes.

Read
Matthew 2:13-18

Sing Together
While most Christmas carols are joyful tunes about the incarnation, the "Coventry Carol" is a haunting melody dedicated to the Holy Innocents. Perhaps listen to it today.

Pray
Say a special prayer of blessing over all your children, celebrating the gift of their lives.
O Lord Jesus Christ, who took little children into your arms and blessed them: Bless the children of this family, [name(s)], that they may grow up in godly fear and love. Give them your strength and guidance day by day, that they may continue in your love and service to their lives' end. Grant this, O blessed Savior, for your own Name's sake. **Amen.**[5]

Feast of the Holy Name of Jesus—January 1

On the eighth day of Christmas, known to most as New Year's Day, the church celebrates the Feast of the Holy Name of Jesus. This celebration remembers that eight days after Christ's birth, he was taken to the synagogue, given the name Jesus, and circumcised according to Jewish custom (Luke 2:21).

As we begin our new calendar year, many people often make resolutions for self-improvement, organization, and self-care. Instead of focusing on ourselves, the church invites us to remember who Jesus is. Let us be reminded this day that Christ calls us by name and gives us new identities: we are chosen, beloved, adopted, precious, known, and seen. Consider which of these identities you want to walk in during the coming year.

Talk to your children about what their names mean and why you gave them their names. Discuss with them a few of the names of Jesus, how he embodied them in the Scriptures, and perhaps how you see his work in your own life related to these names:

1. Jesus ("the Lord saves")
2. Christ/Messiah ("anointed one" or "deliverer")
3. Emmanuel ("God with us")
4. Wonderful Counselor
5. Prince of Peace

Feast of the Holy Family (Moveable)

The feast honoring the Holy Family—Mary, Joseph, and Jesus—is traditionally celebrated on the first Sunday after Christmas. Depending on the year, this could overlap with another feast day or stand on its own. On this day, we remember God's covenant work through families. We remember the faithfulness of Mary and Joseph in receiving the word of God and obeying. We remember the submission of Jesus to his earthly parents, growing in "wisdom and in stature and in favor with God and man" (Luke 2:52) under their care.

It's a good day for setting family goals for the coming calendar year—perhaps a theme verse or word for meditation. Pray through your hopes and anxieties for the year, casting your family cares onto the Lord.

LITURGY FOR CHRISTMAS

Many of the seasonal liturgies in this book have suggestions for weekly readings, but Christmas has daily readings. There are so many wonderful passages for Christmastide. Since there are only twelve days of Christmas and it's a time for feasting on the Lord, I'd encourage you to feast on his Word as a family each day in Christmastide if you're able.

Before you begin, light the Christ candle on your Advent wreath (if you have one) and open your Bible to the week's reading. The words in **bold** are intended for everyone to say together as they are able.

Opening

"Behold, the dwelling place of God is with man. He will dwell with them, and they will be his people, and God himself will be with them as their God" (Revelation 21:3).

Antiphon

The Word was made flesh and dwelt among us:

> **O come, let us adore him.**

The Magnificat (Mary's Song)

Luke 1:46-55

Scripture Reading

Anyone may do the reading. Once the reading has finished, perhaps take a minute to discuss and reflect on it together.

> December 25—Luke 1:1-14
>
> December 26—Acts 6:8-15; 7:54-60
>
> December 27—Mark 1:16-20; John 1:1-18
>
> December 28—Matthew 2:13-18
>
> December 29—Psalm 98
>
> December 30—Titus 3:4-7
>
> December 31—Titus 2:11-14

January 1—Luke 2:15-21

January 2—Psalm 96

January 3—Galatians 3:23–4:7

January 4—Ephesians 1:3-14

January 5—Isaiah 9:1-7

Sing Together
"Joy to the World"

Pray
Take this time to pray as a family, lifting up your own needs and the needs of your community.

Lord's Prayer

Closing Prayer
Almighty God, you have poured upon us the new light of your incarnate Word: Grant that this light, kindled in our hearts, may shine forth in our lives; through Jesus Christ our Lord, who lives and reigns with you in the unity of the Holy Spirit, one God, now and for ever. Amen.[6]

EPIPHANY

I have seen the sun break through
to illuminate a small field
for a while, and gone my way
and forgotten it. But that was the
pearl of great price, the one field that had
treasure in it. I realise now
that I must give all that I have
to possess it. Life is not hurrying
on to a receding future, nor hankering after
an imagined past. It is the turning
aside like Moses to the miracle
of the lit bush, to a brightness
that seemed as transitory as your youth
once, but is the eternity that awaits you.

R.S. THOMAS, "THE BRIGHT FIELD"

STARTS: January 6

ENDS: Fat Tuesday (the day before Ash Wednesday)

TYPE: Proclamation

DISCIPLINE: Prayer and Study of Scripture

NOTABLE DATES:
The Epiphany of Our Lord Jesus
The Presentation of Our Lord Jesus Christ in the Temple (Candlemas)
Saint Valentine's Day

KEY VERSE: "The people who walked in darkness have seen a great light;
those who dwelt in a land of deep darkness, on them has light shone" (Isaiah 9:2).

HYMN: "As with Gladness Men of Old"

FRUIT OF THE SPIRIT: Faithfulness

piphany is the culmination of the Cycle of Light, a season dedicated to the proclamation of God's presence in the world. It begins on January 6 and lasts between six and nine weeks, depending on when Easter falls (and thus, when Lent begins).

History

Epiphany comes from the Latin word *epiphaneia*, meaning "manifestation"—that is, to make known something that was previously hidden. The season of Epiphany in the church marks three major revelations in the life of Christ:

1. The revelation of the gospel to the Gentiles (represented by the journey of the magi)

2. The revelation of Jesus as the Son of God at his baptism

3. The revelation of Jesus's power at the wedding at Cana

While Epiphany is most well-known today as the celebration of the magi, it was originally a feast to remember the baptism of Jesus in the Jordan River. It is unsurprising that the emphasis of Epiphany in the West shifted from Jesus's baptism to the manifestation of salvation to the Gentiles. After all, most Christians in the Western church were not former Jews, but pagan converts. The story of the magi's journey and God's inclusion of all nations to bear witness to and worship the Messiah is a beautiful affirmation of the promise of God being for all people.

Epiphany Places Us in God's Story

The quiet catalyst for the wise men's journey was the emergence of a new star. So great was their faith that upon the appearance of the Christmas star, they selected three gifts of great value, rounded up a caravan, and traveled to an unknown destination in hopes of worshipping the Christ.

The Christian life is a similar pilgrimage—a faith journey that culminates at the pearly gates. Christ is our bright and glorious morning star as we seek, find, and worship the Lord. Calvin's *Institutes* begins with the idea that to know ourselves we must know God, and to know God we must know ourselves. Epiphany invites us into these two knowings. Each step of our journey is an act of trust and an affirmation of faith propelling us "further up and further in"[1] to deeper knowledge of self and God.

In a sense, the season of Epiphany focuses on two types of proclamation:

- An inward proclamation—the annual revelation of Christ with us and a reminder that the journey we're on is leading us ever onward and upward to the City of God.

- An outward proclamation—we bring the good news of God-with-us to all who have ears to hear.

As image bearers of God who take up Christ's specific call to be the light of the world

(Matthew 5:14-16), we are transformed into walking epiphanies, mini-manifestations of God shining forth in the dark world.

Epiphany Is a Spiritual Discipline

Epiphany represents nearly thirty years of Jesus's life, from the visitation of the wise men all the way until Jesus is baptized and spends forty days in the wilderness. We don't know much at all about this period. What the Bible does tell us is that Jesus "increased in wisdom and in stature and in favor with God and man" (Luke 2:52).

In many ways, this phrase captures the essential theme of Epiphany. Our faith journeys should facilitate growth in wisdom and favor with God and man. Epiphany is a perfect season to reboot or renew your commitment to prayer and study of the Word. If regularly engaging these disciplines has been a challenge for you, I suggest you shake up the routine a bit. Here are a few options:

- Commit to joining a small group or Bible study either in person or online.
- Invite a friend (or several) to pray regularly with and for you—phone, Zoom, in person, however you can get it done.
- Practice prayer differently than you usually engage it—try fixed-hour prayer, breath prayer, prayer beads.
- Pray along with prewritten prayers from the Psalms, the Lord's Prayer, other Bible passages, or prayer books.
- Get a journal for recording your Scripture reflections, prayer requests, and the ways you have seen God answer your prayers.
- Commit to memorizing Scripture—the Psalms are especially wonderful for this!
- Create a playlist of Scripture set to music to listen to in the car or at home.
- Find a Bible study or sermon podcast you enjoy and listen while you commute, cook, or complete chores.
- Practice devotional reading (also called *Lectio Divina*).

If you have kids, many of the previous suggestions are things you can also do with them! Pray together during car rides, listen to Scripture music, find a children's prayer or Bible story podcast, or work on memorizing Scripture together.

FIXED-HOUR PRAYER

Fixed-hour prayer is an ancient Jewish practice formalized during the Babylonian captivity. We know from the book of Acts that Jesus's disciples continued these prayer practices even after his ascension.

In the sixth century, Saint Benedict officially structured fixed-hour prayers to be said every three hours, on the hour, over a twenty-four-hour period. This structure is known as the Liturgy of the Hours and the Divine Office. These around-the-clock prayers make a lot of sense for those living within a monastic community. For everyone else, however, the logistics of such a structure are challenging. In her book on spiritual disciplines, Adele Ahlberg Calhoun reformats this structure for the layperson's day:

Waking-up prayer—*Lauds*

Prayer for beginning work—*Prime*

Giving-thanks prayer in midmorning—*Terce*

Noonday prayer of commitment—*Sext*

Midafternoon prayer—*None*

Evening prayer of stillness—*Vespers*

Going-to-sleep prayer of trust—*Compline*[2]

A few notes on praying within this structure:

- Don't start by trying to pray through *all* the hours. Choose one or two times to stop and pray (perhaps set a reminder on your phone).

- Don't put pressure on these prayers to be a space where you pray through *everything* on your heart. Pick one thing to pray for at each hour.

- Keep the time commitment manageable. Even just praying for a literal minute can be a great way to reconnect with God in the midst of a full day.

- Pick a short prayer to read or memorize—the Lord's Prayer or a psalm, for instance—or pray one phrase repeatedly for sixty seconds ("Let your peace guard my heart and mind" or "Send forth your light and truth, let them guide me").

- If you want a longer or more structured time of prayer, you could use the liturgies included in this book or *The Book of Common Prayer*.

Finally, set a reasonable goal for these disciplines and don't make your time with the Lord a box-checking exercise. It's about connecting with God. Remember, God delights to meet with you whenever and however you come to him. If you miss a day (or week) or fall short of your set goal, simply take a breath and come back to the Lord with a short prayer. Our faith journeys are a marathon, not a sprint, and like all spiritual disciplines, prayer and Scripture study are not a requirement for salvation or a way to earn God's love. The ultimate goal is a faith that grows deeper and more intimate year by year, so keep putting one foot in front of the other and walk toward Jesus.

Epiphany Is Communal

The length of Epiphany is determined by the date of Easter and, thus, the start of Lent. If Easter is early, Epiphany may only be forty days, or it could be as long as nine weeks. Epiphany's variability and length make it less full than either Advent or Christmas—there are simply fewer traditions and feast days spread out over a longer period.

Epiphany is the conclusion to the Cycle of Light, and there are six epiphanies remembered in this cycle: the first is to the poor shepherds (December 25), the second to the Gentile magi (January 6), and the third to the righteous elders of Israel (February 2). The fourth epiphany was thirty years later at Jesus's baptism (first Sunday after Epiphany), then the wedding at Cana (second Sunday after Epiphany), and finally the transfiguration (final Sunday after Epiphany).

HOLY HUES

The official color of the Feast of Epiphany is white—the color of joy and purity. But for most of Epiphany, green is used. This is a nod to the season being understood in some traditions as "ordinary time." Green is the color of the Holy Spirit—the color of growth and life—and is an appropriate reminder of the season of Jesus's life in which he grew in wisdom, stature, and favor with God and with man.

Historical Traditions
Twelfth Night

In keeping with the Jewish tradition of beginning the day at sunset the evening before, the Feast of Epiphany begins on the twelfth night of Christmastide, January 5, with a final evening of revelry, rich food, and gift giving. This is an especially apropos date on which to have a party—invite all your friends to bring their leftover Christmas treats, sing carols, and play games! One fun tradition is to have your kids leave their shoes outside the front door on January 5 along with some hay (grass) and water for the magi's camels in order to invite the magi to stop for a visit and bring your kids a gift (or treat!) just like they brought to baby Jesus.

Come January 6, it's time for the magi to arrive at your nativity set—and for your family to enjoy a "king cake" together. Traditionally, this is a ring-shaped cake, frosted and topped with colored sprinkles of gold (for power), green (for faith), and purple (for justice). If you made a traditional Christmas pudding on Stir-Up Sunday, it can definitely sub in for your king cake. Hidden in the cake or pudding is a coin, ring, bean, or little plastic baby. Whoever is served the piece with the token gets to be king or queen for the day. They choose the meals and the entertainment (within reason), and whenever he or she takes a drink, everyone stops and shouts, "The king is drinking!" and must themselves drink. After a few hours of enduring—er, enjoying—one power-drunk child, take a minute to reflect with your family on the humility of the magi, their faithful journey, and their willingness to bow down to a baby, and pray that God may increase your faithfulness and obedience. And of course, don't forget to sing "We Three Kings" (because even though the magi were not really kings, the rest of the lyrics are pretty stellar).

KING CAKE

Servings: slice the cake to serve exactly as many people as are in your party

INGREDIENTS

Pastry:
½ cup milk
2 T. butter
1 (.25 oz.) package (or 2 ¼ tsp) active dry
    yeast
⅓ cup warm water
¼ cup white sugar, divided
1 egg
¾ tsp. salt
¼ tsp. nutmeg
2¼ cups all-purpose flour

Filling:
½ cup packed brown sugar
1½ tsp. ground cinnamon
⅓ cup chopped pecans
¼ cup all-purpose flour
¼ cup butter, melted
Little oven-safe plastic baby doll,
    bean, or quarter

Decoration:
1 cup powdered sugar
1 T. milk
Sprinkles in gold, green, and purple

DIRECTIONS

1. Scald the milk: heat the milk in a saucepan over medium-low heat until tiny bubbles start to appear around the edge of the pan. Remove from the heat and stir in the butter until it melts. Allow the mixture to cool to room temperature.

2. In a large bowl, dissolve the yeast in the warm water with 1 tablespoon of the white sugar. Let it stand about 10 minutes, until foamy.

3. Add the cooled milk mixture to the yeast mixture, then whisk in the egg. Stir in the remaining 3 tablespoons of white sugar, salt, and nutmeg.

4. Beat in the flour 1 cup at a time. When the dough has pulled together, turn it out onto a lightly floured surface and knead until smooth and elastic, about 8 to 10 minutes.

5. Lightly oil a large bowl, place the dough in the bowl, and turn to coat it with oil. Cover with a damp cloth or plastic wrap and let it rise in a warm place until doubled in volume, about 2 hours. When risen, punch down and divide the dough in half.

6. To make the filling, first combine the dry ingredients, then pour in the melted butter and mix until crumbly.

7. Put half the dough on a floured work surface and sprinkle the top with a little additional flour. Roll it into a 10 x 16-inch rectangle. Sprinkle half the filling evenly over the dough and roll it up tightly like a jelly roll, rolling from the longer side. Repeat this process with the other half of the dough, then place the logs on a cookie sheet that has been greased or lined with parchment paper. Arrange the two logs end-to-end to form an oval-shaped ring. With scissors, make cuts at 1-inch intervals to the top of the cake, going only ⅓ of the way down into the dough. Let it rise in a warm spot until doubled in size, about 45 minutes.

8. Preheat the oven to 375°F. Push the doll (or bean or quarter) into the bottom of the cake, taking care that no one will be able to tell where it has been inserted. Then bake for 30 minutes.

9. Prepare a glaze by whisking the powdered sugar and milk together, adding more milk if needed for desired consistency. While the cake is warm, drizzle on the glaze and add the colored sprinkles in a fun pattern.

Chalking the Door

It is among the most ancient of Christian customs to "chalk the door" on the Feast of Epiphany. This tradition may have its roots in the Jewish Passover practice of marking the door with the blood of a lamb. It could also be related to God's command in Deuteronomy 6 to write his Word on the doorposts of their houses. It appears that early Christians appropriated these customs and modified them to contain both a blessing and a reminder.

Each year on Epiphany, a family gathers outside to bless their home, chalking the year and the initials *C*, *M*, and *B* onto their lintel or the top of their front door like this:

$$20 + C + M + B + 24$$

The last two digits change depending on the year (the above example is for the year 2024). *C*, *M*, and *B* likely stand for the Latin phrase *Christus mansionem benedicat*: May Christ bless this house. The + signs are, of course, a symbol of the cross of Christ.

The chalking of the door is first an invitation for Christ to be present in our hearts and homes. It also stands as a reminder to us that our home is a place of refuge and blessing. As the wise men entered the home of Jesus and found welcome, so should all who enter our homes (including ourselves) find Jesus. Our homes are a haven and a space to know and be known by Christ.

Liturgical Traditions
The Feast of the Baptism of Our Lord

While the Feast of Epiphany focuses on the manifestation of the gospel to the Gentiles in the Western tradition, the celebration of the baptism of Jesus follows shortly on its heels. This feast is always observed on the first Sunday after Epiphany.

In the context of Epiphany, the baptism of Jesus is the public revelation of Christ as the Son of God, the promised Messiah. As Jesus emerged from the water, "the heavens were opened to him, and he saw the Spirit of God descending like a dove and coming to rest on him; and behold, a voice from heaven said, 'This is my beloved Son, with whom I am well pleased'" (Matthew 3:16-17).

In Eastern European countries and in most Eastern Orthodox churches, this feast is marked by some daring water activity—jumping into an icy lake, for instance! If you're less brave than our Eastern European brothers and sisters, perhaps settle for a walk near a local body of water just to take in the view, or enjoy your local indoor pool.

Another tradition is to baptize converts to the faith on the Feast of Epiphany. In fact, Advent originally existed as a season to prepare converts for this experience. If you or your children haven't been baptized, prayerfully consider baptism on this day. If you have been baptized, spend some time reflecting on why you were baptized and reaffirm your commitment to Christ and his church.

Candlemas—February 2

This is also known as the Feast of the Presentation of Our Lord Jesus Christ in the Temple. Candlemas marks the last of the "birth narrative" feasts and is considered the finale of the celebration of Christmas. If you still have your nativity set up, this is the day to finally take it down, since Jesus's arrival in his temple signifies the fulfillment of our Advent waiting.

This feast arrives forty days after Christmas and commemorates the day the Holy Family went to the temple in Jerusalem for Mary's ritual purification following childbirth and Jesus's consecration according to the Mosaic covenantal law of the dedication of the first-born son. During this visit, the elderly Simeon and the prophetess Anna recognized the infant Christ for who he is: the promised Savior. Simeon's prayer—now known as the "Nunc Dimittis"—is a beautiful testimony to God's faithfulness and the faith journeys we celebrate in Epiphany (Luke 2:29-32).

As the "light for revelation to the Gentiles," Jesus is especially celebrated this day by blessing a church's entire store of candles for the coming year. Hence, this feast is also known as Candlemas. The Cycle of Light "that began with the successive lighting of the candles of the Advent wreath finds its fulfillment in the blessing and procession with lighted candles in celebration of the arrival of the Lord in his temple."[3] In some traditions, families even bring their own candles to church to be consecrated, a sign of their desire for their home to be a beacon of Christ's light in the coming year. If your local church doesn't bless candles on Candlemas, bless your candles as a family at home!

In celebration of Candlemas, you could go without electric lights for the day, choosing instead to enjoy your home by candlelight. You could also make candles. There are child-friendly beeswax candle kits available if you're looking for something simple.

In France, Candlemas is also known as Crepe Day. Rolled-up crepes also look like candles, and when unrolled, the round, golden crepes look like the sun, a reminder that Jesus is the Light of the World. Perhaps enjoy savory crepes for dinner tonight or sweet crepes for dessert!

DESSERT CREPES

Yield: 8 crepes

INGREDIENTS

Crepes:
4 eggs, lightly beaten
1⅓ cups milk
2 T. butter, melted
1 cup all-purpose flour
2 T. powdered sugar
½ tsp. salt
Oil or butter for pan

Filling Ideas:
Strawberries
Bananas
Nutella
Butter and cinnamon sugar
Whipped cream
Lemon curd and blueberries

DIRECTIONS

1. In a large bowl, whisk together all the crepe ingredients until smooth.

2. Heat a medium-sized skillet or crepe pan over medium heat. Use a brush or paper towel to grease the pan with a small amount of butter or oil. Using a serving spoon or small ladle, spoon about 3 tablespoons of crepe batter into the hot pan, tilting the pan so the bottom surface is evenly coated. Cook 1 to 2 minutes per side, or until golden brown. Serve immediately with your favorite fillings.

NOTE: If you want to make savory crepes, leave the sugar out of this recipe and fill the crepes with your favorite savory items. Suggestions to try: ham, eggs, and cheese; smoked salmon and cream cheese; basil, tomatoes, and fresh mozzarella; turkey and pesto.

Liturgy for Blessing the Candles

Gather some new candles to burn during your family's prayer time for the coming year. The words in **bold** are intended for everyone to say together as they are able.

Antiphon

Our help is the name of the Lord:
The maker of heaven and earth.
Nations shall come to your light
and kings to the brightness of your rising.

Pray

Loving God, who called forth light at the beginning of creation, bless these candles that they may faithfully give light to your people. Let the hearts and minds of all who enter our home be illumined by the true Light of the World. Grant that the light of Christ, once kindled in our hearts, may shine forth in our lives that your glory may be revealed to the ends of the earth; through Jesus Christ our Lord who lives and reigns with you and the Holy Spirit, now and forever. Amen.

Feast of Saint Valentine—February 14

While Valentine's Day is one of the most popular saint days in our culture, very little is known about the man Valentine, and the legends may be a conflation of two different people.

He is said to have been a faithful bishop in Terni, Italy, when Christianity was still illegal. Despite the danger, Valentine passionately shared the gospel and aided persecuted Christians. Supposedly, he also officiated a number of Christian marriages during a time when young men who were drafted into the military were prohibited from marrying. He may also have been a physician. At forty-six, he was arrested by Emperor Claudius and spent some time in prison before being martyred.

One durable legend indicates he became friends with his jailer, Asterius, and his jailer's blind daughter, Julia. Shortly before he was martyred, he sent a farewell letter to Julia to thank her for her friendship and encourage her walk with the Lord. He signed it, "From your Valentine." As the story goes, Julia miraculously regained her sight upon opening this note!

Valentine's Day as we know it now was more than likely (unintentionally) invented by the poet Geoffrey Chaucer in the fourteenth century. In "Parlement of Foules," he writes that Saint Valentine's Day is the annual day on which birds (the "foules") choose their mate. With the popularity of this work also came the popularity of Valentine's Day as a celebration of romance.

The practice of exchanging valentines is done in remembrance of Saint Valentine's faithfulness, courage, and love for others. Take time to write a few notes of kindness to the people you love, and enjoy making valentines with your children. A great passage to read today is 1 Corinthians 13:1-8.

The Transfiguration—Final Sunday of Epiphany

This final Sunday in Epiphany commemorates the transfiguration as a thematic cap-stone to the Cycle of Light, a marker of the last major revelation before the resurrection, in which we read about when Jesus's "face shone like the sun, and his clothes became white as light" (Matthew 17:2). In this moment Peter, James, and John behold Jesus's true glory. We seek to join with these disciples in looking upon the light of Christ, praying that God would "grant that we, beholding by faith the light of his countenance, may be strengthened to bear our cross, and be changed into his likeness from glory to glory."[4]

Preparing for Lent

Lent begins directly after Epiphany and marks a sharp change to the church year in both tone and practice. These final weeks of Epiphany are a good time to plan for how you want to observe Lent: Will you fast? Will you add prayer practices? How will your family participate in the season?

Burying the Alleluia

One Epiphanic tradition designed to prepare our hearts for Lent is the burying of the alleluia. Since the fifth century, it has been the tradition to eliminate the joyful "alleluia" from the worship service during Lent. It is not sung or said.

In the Middle Ages, it became customary to literally bury the alleluia—that is, to "place it in a tomb" that it may be "resurrected" at Easter. Sometimes this is done the last Sunday of Epiphany by the church congregation and sometimes by individuals and families on Fat Tuesday. It is a great activity to help your children mark the shift from one season to another.

Simply take a long piece of paper and write "Alleluia!" on it. Decorate it as brightly and joyfully as you can. Then fold it or roll it up, put it in a plastic bag, and bury it in your yard. Don't forget where you put it! On Easter, dig it up and display it. Christ is risen and with him our great joy and praise.

LITURGY FOR EPIPHANY

For the season of Epiphany, I have included readings for each Sunday after Epiphany. If you're looking for readings for the days between Sundays, I strongly suggest using this season and the weeks of Lent to read through one of the Gospels together as a family. These weeks leading up to Easter are ideal for meditating on the life of Christ.

Please note that because Easter is a moveable feast, you may not end up using all the included readings. Regardless, the final Sunday in Epiphany is always the reading of the transfiguration.

Before you begin, light a candle and open your Bible to the week's reading. The words in **bold** are intended for everyone to say together as they are able.

Opening
"Nations shall come to your light, and kings to the brightness of your rising" (Isaiah 60:3).

Antiphon
The Lord has shown forth his glory:
> **O come, let us adore him.**

Nunc Dimittis (Simeon's Song)
Luke 2:29-32

Scripture Reading
Anyone may do the reading. Once the reading has finished, perhaps take a minute to discuss and reflect on it together.

1. January 6 (Epiphany)—Matthew 2:1-12
2. First Sunday after Epiphany—Matthew 3:13-17
3. Second Sunday after Epiphany— John 2:1-11
4. Third Sunday after Epiphany—Mark 1:14-20
5. Fourth Sunday after Epiphany—Matthew 5:1-12
6. February 2 (Candlemas)—Luke 2:22-40

7. Fifth Sunday after Epiphany—Matthew 5:13-20

8. Sixth Sunday after Epiphany—Mark 1:40-45

9. Seventh Sunday after Epiphany—Mark 2:1-12

10. Eighth Sunday after Epiphany— Matthew 9:35-38

11. The Last Sunday of Epiphany—Matthew 17:1-9

Sing Together
"As with Gladness Men of Old"

Pray
Take this time to pray as a family, lifting up your own needs and the needs of your community.

Lord's Prayer

Closing Prayer
Give us grace, O Lord, to answer readily the call of our Savior Jesus Christ and proclaim to all people the Good News of his salvation, that we and the whole world may perceive the glory of his marvelous works; who lives and reigns with you and the Holy Spirit, one God, for ever and ever. Amen.[5]

FAT TUESDAY

Let us eat and drink, for tomorrow we die.

ISAIAH 22:13

Before turning our hearts to the penitential season of Lent and its accompanying Lenten fast, Christians have traditionally celebrated one final hurrah known as Fat Tuesday. This day—which immediately precedes Ash Wednesday—is also known as Shrove Tuesday, Pancake Day, and Mardi Gras (French for Fat Tuesday).

Historically, Fat Tuesday was "fat" because it was a time to eat up all your rich, fatty foods before beginning the great fast of Lent. Often this meant combining your eggs, butter, and milk with flour to make pancakes (and don't forget the bacon and sausage to go with it). Fat Tuesday is a unique feast in the church year in that it's technically not on the liturgical calendar or formally recognized by the church at all. It's a tradition that mostly sprouted up out of the desire not to waste food, so this feast day is actually just good stewardship!

One lesser-known name for Fat Tuesday is Shrove Tuesday. The word *shrove* derives from *shrive*: to present oneself for confession and absolution. This name originates from the ancient tradition of readying oneself for Lent through self-examination and confession. Learn more about confession on page 131.

Fat Tuesday is celebrated across the world in a variety of ways. In some cultures, the spirit of Fat Tuesday was extended into an entire debaucherous season known sometimes as Carnival or Mardi Gras (this is why in New Orleans, king cakes are consumed from January 6 all the way until Lent). *Carnival* comes from the Latin *carne vale*, meaning "farewell to meat." For most communities, Fat Tuesday is all about the food:

- In France, they celebrate with crepes, waffles, and *beignets*.
- In Portugal and Hawaii, they eat *malasadas* (sugar-coated donuts).
- In Poland and Polish communities, they eat deep-fried, jelly-filled donuts called *paczkis*.
- In Italy, it's all about the *cannoli*.
- In Spain, it's omelet day.
- In Sweden, they eat *semlor* (a treat akin to a cream puff).
- In Ireland and the United Kingdom, it's all about the pancakes. In some towns, they even have pancake races wherein a runner must flip a pancake in a pan while running. This might be a fun activity with your kids.

All this to say, on Fat Tuesday, feel free to indulge a bit in something decadent and delicious!

These Fat Tuesday traditions also assume that a person will be giving up a particular food (meat, alcohol, and/or sweets) for Lent. If you choose to give up something different for Lent—television or social media, for instance—then you may opt to indulge in those things on Fat Tuesday.

BUTTERMILK PANCAKES

These pancakes are fluffy and delicious. To make them extra-special, sprinkle some chocolate chips into the batter before cooking. If you don't have buttermilk, add 1 tablespoon of white vinegar or lemon juice to one cup of milk and let the mixture sit for five minutes before using.

Servings: 4

INGREDIENTS

2 cups all-purpose flour
¼ cup sugar
2¼ tsp. baking powder
½ tsp. baking soda
½ tsp. salt
2 eggs
2 cups buttermilk
¼ cup unsalted butter, melted

DIRECTIONS

1. Add the dry ingredients to a large bowl and mix well to combine.

2. In a small bowl, beat the eggs and buttermilk together with a whisk. Slowly pour in the melted butter, whisking constantly to avoid cooking the eggs.

3. Pour the wet ingredients into the dry and mix gently with a spoon until just moistened. Do not overmix! The batter should still have lumps.

4. Heat a griddle or skillet over medium-low heat and add ⅓ cup of batter. Cook the pancakes 2 to 3 minutes on the first side, or until the edges look slightly dry and bubbles begin to form on top. Flip the pancakes and cook another 1 to 2 minutes. Serve with butter and syrup or berries and whipped cream.

Adapted with gratitude from Liz Flourez, Love Grows Wild.

CYCLE OF LIFE
GOD FOR US

Look at the birds
Consider the lilies
Drink ye all of it
Ask
Seek
Knock
Enter by the narrow gate
Do not be anxious
Judge not; do not give dogs what is holy
Go: be it done for you
Do not be afraid
Maiden, arise
Young man, I say, arise
Stretch out your hand
Stand up, be still
Rise, let us be going...
Love
Forgive
Remember me

KATHLEEN NORRIS,
"IMPERATIVES, PART 2 OF MYSTERIES OF THE INCARNATION"

ASH WEDNESDAY

The people of Israel were assembled with fasting and in sackcloth, and with earth on their heads. And the Israelites separated themselves from all foreigners and stood and confessed their sins and the iniquities of their fathers.

NEHEMIAH 9:1-2

On Ash Wednesday we enter the second cycle of the Christian year, known as the Cycle of Life, in which we remember Christ *for* us. This cycle contains the same three movements as the Cycle of Light: preparation (Lent, which includes Holy Week), celebration (Easter), and proclamation (Ordinary Time).

Ash Wednesday kicks off the penitential season of Lent. This day is one of the few official church holy days that has no relation to the life of Christ. Up until now, the Church's seasons flow naturally from one to another—we wait, Christ arrives, we celebrate, the magi come, we seek the Lord and proclaim his work, and then all of a sudden Ash Wednesday gets tossed in the mix like a bucket of icy water. In many ways, that's exactly what it's designed to be: a wake-up call. It points out that we are still sinners heading for death and admonishes us to repent, fix our eyes on the cross, and pray for mercy.

On this day, millions of Christians across the globe gather to repent, pray, fast, and have ashes placed on their foreheads in the shape of the cross. Initially, the imposition of ashes was only for those who, because of their sins, were separated from the church and were now seeking restoration to the body of Christ. The ashes marked the start of the reconciliation process. By the tenth century, it was standard for all Christians to receive ashes

in solidarity with the penitent and as a reminder that death is the great equalizer—notorious sinner or renowned saint, both from dust to dust.

Each year, the ashes are made from the palm fronds of the previous year's Palm Sunday procession. Burned down to dust, mixed with holy oil,[1] and imposed on foreheads, the palms are a reminder that what was once vivid and lively decays into something frail, brittle, and eventually indistinguishable from the earth itself. Fundamentally, it's a symbol of God's judgment and the grievous effect of sin. As the priest places the ashes on the forehead in the shape of a cross, he pronounces the condemnation of Genesis 3: "Remember that you are dust, and to dust you shall return."

But while ashes are a sign of mourning and penitence, they are also a symbol of purification. In ancient times, ashes were used for scouring something clean in the absence of soap. There is paradox in the ashes as there is paradox in the waters of baptism—by water we die and by water we are washed clean, by ashes we repent and by ashes we are renewed.

Yes, we came from dust and yes, we shall return to dust again, but *oh, what glorious things* God can do with dust! God, who lovingly shaped man from dust and breathed his very life into that dust, has promised to lovingly reshape our dust and breathe life into us again too. Even as the ashes are a reminder of our inevitable death, we do not despair. After all, death is just a prerequisite for resurrection. Let us have faith in what dust can be in the hands of a loving God.

Ash Wednesday and the whole Lenten season invite us to sit in the tension of sickness and cure, sin and redemption, death and resurrection. Lent calls upon the promises of God in Isaiah 61:3 that in Christ we will experience transformation: "a crown of beauty instead of ashes, the oil of joy instead of mourning, and a garment of praise instead of a spirit of despair" (NIV). In this season, we make an offering to God of our own dust—our selfish desires, our escapist habits, our earthly indulgences and dependencies, our bodies, appetites, time, and money—and we ask the Lord to make beauty from ashes.

All those days
you felt like dust,
like dirt,
as if all you had to do
was turn your face
toward the wind
and be scattered
to the four corners

or swept away
by the smallest breath
as insubstantial—

did you not know
what the Holy One
can do with dust?

This is the day
we freely say
we are scorched.

This is the hour
we are marked
by what has made it
through the burning.

This is the moment
we ask for the blessing
that lives within
the ancient ashes,
that makes its home
inside the soil of
this sacred earth.

So let us be marked
not for sorrow.
And let us be marked
not for shame.
Let us be marked
not for false humility
or for thinking
we are less
than we are

but for claiming
what God can do
within the dust,
within the dirt,
within the stuff
of which the world
is made
and the stars that blaze
in our bones
and the galaxies that spiral
inside the smudge
we bear.

JAN RICHARDSON, "BLESSING THE DUST"

Observing Ash Wednesday

Worship

Go to church on Ash Wednesday and receive ashes. Wear your ashes as long as you are comfortable doing so. Some people prefer to wear theirs all day as a public witness ("Hey, there's something on your head" is an oft-heard conversation starter on Ash Wednesday). Others prefer to remove their ashes so as not to appear more holy than those they encounter throughout their day. If you're unable to make it to church, spend time today confessing, repenting, and praying.

Fast

If it is safe for you to do so, abstain from food from waking until sundown. Alternately, fast by eating very lightly until dinner. Even if your chosen Lenten fast is from something other than food, Ash Wednesday is an appropriate day to abstain from eating in order to focus your heart and mind on prayer and repentance.

Pray

The liturgy for Lent on pages 123-125 is appropriate for Ash Wednesday and includes suggested readings for this day.

Almighty and everlasting God, you hate nothing you have made, and you forgive the sins of all who are penitent: Create and make in us new and contrite hearts, that we, worthily lamenting our sins and acknowledging our wretchedness, may obtain of you, the God of all mercy, perfect remission and forgiveness; through Jesus Christ our Lord, who lives and reigns with you and the Holy Spirit, one God, for ever and ever. **Amen.**[2]

LENT

Repeat. Do you read? Do you read? Are you in trouble? How did you get in trouble?
If you are in trouble, have you sought help? If you did, did help come? If it did, did you accept it?
Are you out of trouble? What is the character of your consciousness? Are you conscious?
Do you have a self? Do you know who you are? Do you know what you're doing? Do you love?
Do you know how to love? Are you loved? Do you hate? Do you read me? Come back. Repeat. Come back.
Come back. Come back.

WALKER PERCY, *LOST IN THE COSMOS*

STARTS: Ash Wednesday

ENDS: Holy Saturday (the day before Easter)

TYPE: Preparation

DISCIPLINE: Fasting, Prayer, and Almsgiving

NOTABLE DATES:
Ash Wednesday
Saint Patrick's Day
Feast of the Annunciation
Laetare Sunday
Holy Week and the Triduum[1]

KEY VERSE: "'Yet even now,' declares the LORD, 'return to me with all your heart, with fasting, with weeping, and with mourning; and rend your hearts and not your garments.' Return to the LORD your God, for he is gracious and merciful, slow to anger, and abounding in steadfast love; and he relents over disaster" (Joel 2:12-13).

HYMN: "Guide Me, O Thou Great Jehovah"

FRUIT OF THE SPIRIT: Self-Control

Lent begins on Ash Wednesday and ends on Holy Saturday (the Saturday before Easter Sunday). Some years it's as early as Saint Valentine's Day, and other years it's as late as March 10. A quick google will tell you the date each year. Lent is understood as a forty-day fast, but between Ash Wednesday and Holy Saturday there are actually forty-six days. Here's why: Sundays are not counted as a part of Lent. On Sundays we gather to worship, to celebrate the resurrection and partake of the feast of Communion. Sundays are for feasting—always, in every season—and so cannot be counted as part of the Lenten fast.

The term *Lent* comes from the old English *lencten*, meaning "lengthen"—a description of the increasingly longer days that characterize spring. While Lent literally happens in the spring (at least in the Northern Hemisphere), the name also symbolizes the awakening and growth called forth in the life of the Christian. Lent invites us to contemplate the connections between winter and spring, death and resurrection, and how self-denial makes our hearts fertile growing places for the seeds of faith.

History

From its inception, Lent was designed to assist Christian communities in preparing their hearts to celebrate the resurrection by facilitating a season of reflection and penitence aided by fasting. The original "Lent" is said by Augustine and Tertullian to have been observed by the apostles themselves.[2] But for the early church it was a forty-*hour* fast to commemorate the time from Christ's death (Friday, 3:00 p.m.) to his resurrection (Sunday, 7:00 a.m.). At the end of these forty hours, of course, the church gathered for the Feast of Easter.

As the church expanded beyond Jerusalem, it became customary for Christians to take a pilgrimage to the blessed city for the Easter feast. At that point, the start of Lent was shifted to Palm Sunday for those who wished to relive Jesus's final week.[3] Eventually Lent was extended to three weeks to give time to prepare baptismal candidates, and then, by the early third century, it was extended to forty days. These forty days are a mirror of Christ's forty days in the desert.

Lent Places Us in God's Story

Forty is a significant number in the life of God's people: The Lord flooded the earth for forty days; Moses was on Mount Sinai for forty days; the Israelites wandered the desert for forty years; and Jesus spent forty days in the wilderness before he began his ministry, as well as forty days with his disciples between his resurrection and ascension. The forty days of Lent, then, place us not only in the story of Christ's life but also in the story of God's people. In the Bible, forty symbolizes the fullness of time. The common thread of each of these stories is God's transforming work to prepare his people for what's next.

While the themes of Epiphany orient our hearts to sacred pilgrimage, Lent pushes us

HOLY HUES

The official color of Lent is violet or purple, as it is during Advent. When used within the church, purple is traditionally the color of penitence and mourning. Purple was chosen because it is made by mixing blue (the color of hope) and red (the color of blood and of God's love). While our penitence is sincere because we know the Lord is grieved by our sin, we repent with hope because we've been bought by the blood of Jesus. The color purple signifies the contrition of the redeemed.

out into the desert as a reminder that wandering, too, is holy. In the ebb and flow of the Christian life, most of us experience seasons when we feel we've drifted from the path, or the path has just disappeared, or we've beaten our own path in what we hope is the right direction because *what other choice do we have?*

Wandering seasons are as essential to the life of God's people as purposeful pilgrimages. Graham Cooke says wandering seasons have the ability to "connect us with God's wisdom, and wisdom is the revelation of who God is and the internal recognition of how He likes to work in our lives.... It is about understanding the deep things of God."[4] As we wander, we're apt to discover unexpected ways God continues to pursue us, our good, our growth, our love, and our holiness.

> Not all those who wander are lost.
>
> J.R.R. Tolkien, *The Fellowship of the Ring*

After his baptism, Jesus is driven by the Spirit deep into the wilderness for his own season of wandering. It is at this moment of Christ's life that we join him on Ash Wednesday. For forty days in the wilderness, Jesus not only fasts from food, but he relinquishes the glory and the power that could have come after his baptism. There were perhaps hundreds or even thousands of people who bore witness to that event[5]—who heard the voice of God and watched the dove descend. Because of the epiphany at the Jordan River, Jesus could have been an instant sensation with a giant platform and a massive group of disciples. Instead, he vanished into the wilderness and wasn't seen again publicly for several weeks or even months.

Of Jesus's time in the desert, Matthew writes, "And after fasting forty days and forty nights, he was hungry" (4:2). A fast will make us hungry, and hunger isn't just for food—it can be for success, power, relationship, wealth, or innumerable other things. When Jesus was hungry, Satan came. He asked, "Aren't you hungry for bread? Hungry to prove your power? Hungry for dominion over this world?" Or, to recall Genesis 3, "Aren't you hungry to be like God?"[6] This temptation proved to be too much for Adam and Eve, but Jesus rejected these offers of godlike power and glory apart from unity with God the Father. By the power of the Holy Spirit, Jesus—the second Adam—overcame where the first Adam failed.

As we approach Lent and prepare our hearts for Easter by fasting and prayer, we are invited to share in Christ's power to overcome. Through his death and resurrection, we are new creations, and with the help of the Holy Spirit, we are capable of communing with the Father, understanding his revelation, and resisting the temptation to sin. Lent invites us to make Jesus's powerful season of desert wandering present in our own lives while living into the future promise of our full restoration.

Lent Is a Spiritual Discipline

Lent is the only season of the church year that has an officially assigned spiritual discipline. In fact, it has three. The three pillars of Lent are fasting, prayer, and almsgiving. These are taken from Jesus's Sermon on the Mount and his three "When you..." statements:

1. "When you give to the needy..." (Matthew 6:2)
2. "When you pray..." (Matthew 6:5)
3. "When you fast..." (Matthew 6:16)

Alms comes from an old English word meaning compassion or mercy, and it has become the practice of the church to particularly attend to the poor and the needy during the season of Lent.

In the context of Lent, prayer and almsgiving naturally flow from fasting. As we tithe our money to enable ministry and tithe our time (Sabbath) to enable worship and rest, we tithe our appetites to make space in our budget to give and in our days to pray. These three practices are also considered symbols of restored relationship:

- With God (prayer), we are free to enter God's presence and be in ceaseless communication with him.
- With man (almsgiving), we are free to put the needs of others ahead of our own.
- With self (fasting), we are free from our appetites and desires.

The primary purpose of the Lenten fast is to allow you to hunger and thus to seek God for satisfaction and strength. Lynne Baab's explanation of fasting is perhaps the most helpful: "Christian fasting is the voluntary denial of something for a specific time, for a spiritual purpose, by an individual, family, community or nation."[7] In this day and age, our appetites and indulgences often go beyond our caloric consumption. Things like shopping, television, social media, podcasts, and exercise can devour our time, drain our bank accounts, distract our hearts, and displace our prayers. None of these things are inherently bad—indeed, many are good gifts! But giving them up for a season to prioritize worship and prayer is a great way to build healthier spiritual habits and deepen our relationship with the Lord.

The focus of a Lenten fast is *not*

- punishment (a fast should be challenging but not miserable),
- a way of atoning for your sins (Jesus already did that),
- weight loss (if a change in eating habits is focused on self instead of the Lord, it is simply a diet),
- a chance to reboot New Year's resolutions (feel free to get back on that wagon, but that is not the meaning of a Lenten fast),
- an opportunity to break habits.

Remember, whatever you give up for Lent is something you should be able to enjoy *again* after Lent is over as well as on Sundays during Lent.

Traditionally, the churchwide Lenten fast called on parishioners to abstain from meat and animal products like eggs and dairy, and to limit the daily intake of food to a light breakfast, one half-meal, and one full meal per day. Younger children (under thirteen), pregnant and nursing women, the sick, and the elderly were exempt from these expectations.

FUN FACT

While Lent can be challenging, it's not without its treats. Soft pretzels are, in fact, traditionally consumed during Lent. Composed primarily of water, salt, yeast, and flour, pretzels adhere to the food abstinence boundaries of the traditional fast. In the fifth century, the soft pretzel was devised as a Lenten snack, and these delicious treats only made a public appearance between Ash Wednesday and Good Friday each year. *Pretzel* comes from the German *bretzal*, which is from the Latin *bracellae*, meaning "little arms." Indeed, the pretzel looks like arms crossed in prayer or to receive a blessing. You can make this treat using the recipe on page 115.

One year, the conservative in me had a strong sense that joining in this traditional fast was the most sensible and communally supportive discipline I could choose for Lent. After two weeks, I was wretched. I was spending all my time trying to find new recipes, and going vegan didn't fit the tastes or budget of my family of five. For me, the traditional fast accomplished the opposite of its intended purpose; I had no additional time for prayer or money for giving!

Based on this experience, my recommendation is for each person (or family) to prayerfully determine what kind of fast would be most spiritually beneficially to you each season. The purpose of fasting is to increase our awareness of specific spiritual blockages that prevent God from acting freely in and through us.[8] To that end, consider these questions when trying to determine what you will fast from during Lent:

1. "When I'm tired or stressed, what things do I turn to in order to help me relax, decompress, or escape?"

2. "Do I routinely make nonessential purchases that could be ceased for a time in order to redirect that money to those in need?"

3. "When I consider my daily routine, what are my favorite parts of my day? Do I love those things more than I love my time with the Lord?"

Honest answers to these questions will likely yield an idea of what you are being called to give up for Lent. Once you determine what you're giving up, ask two more questions:

1. "How will giving up this thing make more space in my life for prayer?" When you're craving the thing from which you're fasting, pray that God's power would be made perfect in your weakness (2 Corinthians 12:9). Lent is a perfect season to commit to a new prayer practice.[9]

2. "How will giving up this thing make more space in my budget for almsgiving?" Almsgiving is giving beyond your normal tithe, and the practice comes from Isaiah 58. The tradition of almsgiving during Lent expands the focus of fasting from a personal spiritual experience to a compassionate communal sacrifice.

SOFT PRETZELS

Yield: 8 pretzels

INGREDIENTS

For the dough:
1½ cups warm (not hot) water
1 T. sugar
2 tsp. salt
1 (.25 oz) package active dry yeast
4½ to 5 cups all-purpose flour
4 T. butter, melted

To cook:
Vegetable oil, for pan
10 cups water
⅔ cup baking soda
1 large egg yolk beaten with 1 T. water
Coarse-grained salt

DIRECTIONS

1. Make the dough: Combine the water, sugar, and kosher salt in the bowl of a stand mixer and sprinkle the yeast on top. Allow it to sit for 5 minutes or until the mixture begins to foam. Add 4½ cups of flour and the butter. Using the dough hook attachment, mix on low speed until well combined. Change to medium speed and knead until the dough is smooth and pulls away from the sides of the bowl, approximately 4 to 5 minutes. (Note: an additional ¼ to ½ cup of flour may be necessary during kneading if you are not using a stand-mixer.) Remove the dough from the bowl, clean the bowl, and then oil it well with vegetable oil. Return the dough to the bowl, cover it with plastic wrap, and let it sit in a warm place for approximately one hour, or until the dough has doubled in size.

2. Preheat the oven to 450°F. Line 2 baking sheets with parchment paper and lightly brush with the vegetable oil. Set aside.

3. In a large pot, bring the water and baking soda to a rolling boil.

4. In the meantime, turn the dough out onto a slightly oiled work surface and divide it into 8 equal pieces. Roll out each piece of dough into a 24-inch rope. Make a U-shape with each rope, holding the ends, then cross them over each other and press them onto the bottom of the U to form the shape of a pretzel. Place them on the parchment-lined half-sheet pans.

5. Place the pretzels in the boiling water, one by one, for 30 seconds. Remove them from the water using a large, flat spatula. Return each pretzel to the baking sheet, brush the top with the egg-yolk-and-water mixture and sprinkle with the coarse salt. When all the pretzels have been boiled, bake them until dark golden brown, approximately 12 to 14 minutes. Transfer to a cooling rack for at least 5 minutes before serving.

Adapted with gratitude from Alton Brown

FASTING FROM FOOD DURING LENT

The Lenten fast is designed to encourage holiness and spiritual health.
With that in mind, do not fast from food for Lent if you

- struggle or have struggled with an eating disorder;
- compulsively diet, obsessively exercise, or have significant body-image issues;
- are tempted to make it about losing weight, changing your figure, or improving your eating habits.

Three Guidelines for Your Fast

1. **Don't talk about the fast (and especially don't complain about it).** Your chosen Lenten fast is private information (Matthew 6:17-18). In fact, if it comes to a choice between breaking your fast and talking about your fast, I say always break your fast.

2. **Don't fast on Sundays.** Sundays are always, in all seasons, a feast day. It is the day of our Lord's resurrection and the day we partake of the feast of Communion. Taste and see that the Lord is good! Especially if you have kids, making or buying a special dessert every Sunday during Lent is a wonderful way to catch the spirit of a feast day!

3. **Fast for the right reasons.** Do not fast out of a sense of pride, legalism, or guilt. Fasting, like all spiritual disciplines, is an optional enhancement to your spiritual life and strongly recommended, but not an obligation.

"Let us fast then, whenever we see fit, and as strenuously as we should.
But having gotten that exercise out of the way, let us *eat*."

ROBERT FARRAR CAPON, *THE SUPPER OF THE LAMB*

PRACTICING THE THREE PILLARS OF LENT WITH KIDS

Obviously, expecting children to fast for forty days from *any-thing* is unrealistic and potentially unhealthy, especially if they don't have a proper theological understanding of what they are doing and why. But fasting, prayer, and almsgiving are all practices children (starting around age four or five) can be capable of with the right preparation and parameters.

Sit down with your kids and brainstorm ways you might participate in the three pillars as a family. One option is to focus on one discipline per two weeks of Lent. For the first and fourth weeks, focus on fasting. For the second and fifth weeks, almsgiving. For the third and sixth weeks, prayer.

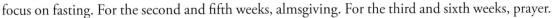

Fasting
You could collaboratively decide on six one-day fasts—one per week during Lent. These can be things like fasting from desserts, television or movies, drinks other than water, games, and so on. Alternately, choose to fast from one thing for a whole week at a time or choose to fast from one thing per day. Remind your children of the fast the night before and remind them why you're fasting. When the moment arrives that they want whatever they're fasting from, pray with them and gently redirect them.

Prayer
Consider doing a memorization project during Lent. Pick one verse per week, or something longer to work on through the whole of the season. Some great options are Psalm 51, Psalm 121, the Lord's Prayer, the Ten Commandments, or the Apostles' Creed. Commit to doing morning or evening prayer together a few times per week using the liturgy for Lent included in this chapter. Set a realistic goal. If every night isn't possible, aim for two or three times per week.

Almsgiving
Offer your children opportunities to do extra chores to earn money they can give away. Keep an "Almsgiving Jar" where they can see it. Additionally, take this opportunity to clean out unused toys and donate them to a local charity. Other ideas for almsgiving include making blessing bags for the homeless, baking treats to give neighbors or teachers, or taking on an extra volunteer role at church or in a local community organization.

Lent Is Communal
Lent in Your Home

While *decorating* might be the wrong term to use for this season, there are ways you can prepare your home to facilitate meditation on simplicity, wilderness, and repentance during the weeks of Lent.

- **Prepare your table**—cover it with a purple tablecloth or table runner or a rough fabric like burlap. Undyed linen is commonly used during Lent as well. Place a vase or other centerpiece of dead sticks on the table.

- **Lenten candles**—another option for adorning your table is to place seven violet candles on it in the shape of a cross. This functions like a reverse Advent wreath. At the start of Lent, you light all seven candles. Then each successive Sunday, you blow out one additional candle until finally, on Maundy Thursday, you extinguish the final (center) candle. As the darkness deepens each week, we are reminded of Christ's journey to Golgotha.

- **Burn a scented candle**—myrrh, sandalwood, balsam, and cedarwood oils were all used to prepare bodies for burial. Allow these scents to become the "smell of Lent" in your home.

- **Make a paper chain**—help your children count down to Easter by creating a paper chain. Use purple for weekdays and Saturday. Use white or gold for Sundays and Easter. Use black for Ash Wednesday, Good Friday, and Holy Saturday.

- **Fast of the eyes**—during the season of Lent, it is typical for churches to engage in what's known as the "Fast of the Eyes," where crosses, crucifixes, statues, and icons of Christ are shrouded in a purple or black cloth. If you have any of these items on display in your home, consider covering them during Lent.

- **Observe the Friday fast**—every Friday through the entire church year is designated as a day of abstinence from meat unless a major feast or holiday falls on this day. This is in remembrance of Christ being crucified on a Friday. Lent can be a great time to dip your toe in the water. For my family, this often means homemade meatless pizza Fridays, but we also love a simple meal of soup and bread.

- **Observe the Sunday feast**—enjoy a delicious dessert on Sundays with your family. Some easy options are ice cream sundaes or fresh berries with a large dollop of whipped cream.

Praying the Decalogue

The Decalogue is a responsive way of praying through the Ten Commandments. While Jesus fulfilled the ceremonial requirements of the law, he spent much of his time on earth teaching about the moral law and how to obey it in spirit and in truth. During the season of Lent, it is customary to pray the Decalogue and ask for God's grace to obey these laws. If you or your children haven't memorized the Ten Commandments, Lent is a perfect time to learn this essential summary of God's law. The Decalogue is included in the Lenten liturgy.

Ember Days

Each season of the year includes a set of Ember Days. In spring this is always the Wednesday, Friday, and Saturday after the first Sunday in Lent. These are days for fasting and praying for your pastor or priest and lay ministers as they faithfully steward your congregation. For additional information on Ember Days, see page 181.

Feast of Saint Patrick

When Patrick was a young man living in Roman Britain, he was abducted by Irish pirates and sold into slavery. Though his father was a deacon and his grandfather a bishop, it was really in the sheep fields of Ireland that Patrick found God. One night, he had a dream in which God told Patrick a ship was ready to take him home. Two hundred miles from the nearest coast, Patrick ran away from his master, traveled to the sea, and found the promised vessel. Eventually, Patrick was reunited with his family and took up the study of theology.

One night he had another dream in which he was handed a letter from the people of Ireland. Patrick writes in his *Confessions*, "As I started to read it was as if I could hear the voices of the people.... 'We implore you, O holy boy, to come here and be with us.'"[10] Once his studies were complete, he returned to the Emerald Isle as an ambassador for Christ.

Unsurprisingly, his knowledge of the Irish language and Irish pagan beliefs made Patrick an excellent missionary. With his love for the people of Ireland and his passion for the Lord, Patrick was incredibly successful in sharing the gospel. Over his thirty-six years in ministry, he baptized thousands of people, founded dozens of churches across Ireland, and trained and ordained at least as many priests. Today he is the patron saint of Ireland, and his day is extravagantly celebrated both in Ireland and Irish American enclaves on March 17.

Celebrating Saint Patrick

Though often used as an excuse for mischief and drunkenness, Saint Patrick's Day can still be observed in fun and festive ways that honor Patrick's bold proclamation of the gospel. At this point, many of the traditions surrounding Saint Patrick's Day revolve more broadly around a celebration of Irish traditions. But considering how much Patrick loved the Irish, this isn't necessarily a bad thing.

Pray

Other than his Trinity shamrock, Patrick is probably best known for the lengthy prayer entitled "Saint Patrick's Breastplate." The most famous portion is this:

> Christ with me,
> Christ before me,
> Christ behind me,
> Christ in me,
> Christ beneath me,
> Christ above me,
> Christ on my right,
> Christ on my left,
> Christ when I lie down,
> Christ when I sit down,
> Christ when I arise,
> Christ in the heart of every man who thinks of me,
> Christ in the mouth of everyone who speaks of me,
> Christ in every eye that sees me,
> Christ in every ear that hears me.

This prayer, especially fun to act out with children, is such a wonderful reminder of Christ's presence and faithfulness. Pray it together as a family today, and perhaps make it one of your memorization projects for Lent.

Feast

While Saint Patrick's Day is during Lent, there are plenty of excellent food and drink choices even for those with very stringent food-related fasts. Our family favorite is potato soup.

Feast of the Annunciation

Since the fifth century, March 25 has been set aside for the memorial and celebration of the archangel Gabriel's appearance to Mary, when he invited her to partner with God in the birth of his Son. Mary was chosen to bear the hope of the world, and her final response to this overwhelming news was "I am the servant of the Lord; let it be to me according to your word" (Luke 1:38). At the Feast of the Annunciation, we remember Mary's "yes" to God. By her obedience, the very Word of God became flesh and dwelt among us. That is worthy of celebration!

Celebrating the Annunciation

Read

The account of the Annunciation is in Luke 1:26-28.

Pray

Pour your grace into our hearts, O Lord, that we who have known the incarnation of your Son Jesus Christ, announced by an angel to the Virgin Mary, may by his cross and passion be brought to the glory of his resurrection; who lives and reigns with you, in the unity of the Holy Spirit, one God, now and forever. **Amen.**[11]

Praying the Magnificat (Luke 1:46-55) would be appropriate as well.

Eat

This feast day is more commonly known as Lady Day, as Mary is frequently referred to as "Our Lady" in certain traditions. In Swedish, "Our Lady's Day" is *Vårfrudagen*. This sounds an awful lot like their word for "Waffle Day," which is *Våffeldagen*. And thus, the tradition of waffles to mark the Feast of the Annunciation was born.

Laetare Sunday

Laetare Sunday is the fourth Sunday in Lent and the counterpart of Advent's Gaudete Sunday. Like the word *gaudete*, *laetare* is Latin for "rejoice!" While *gaudete* denotes an inward state of joy, *laetare* is focused on an outward demonstration. This Sunday serves as encouragement to persevere—Lent is nearly over! On this day the liturgical color shifts to rose, representing a lightening of our darkness, and joy in the midst of penitence. You can celebrate by using a rose-colored candle for your Lenten candle cross or wearing pink to church.

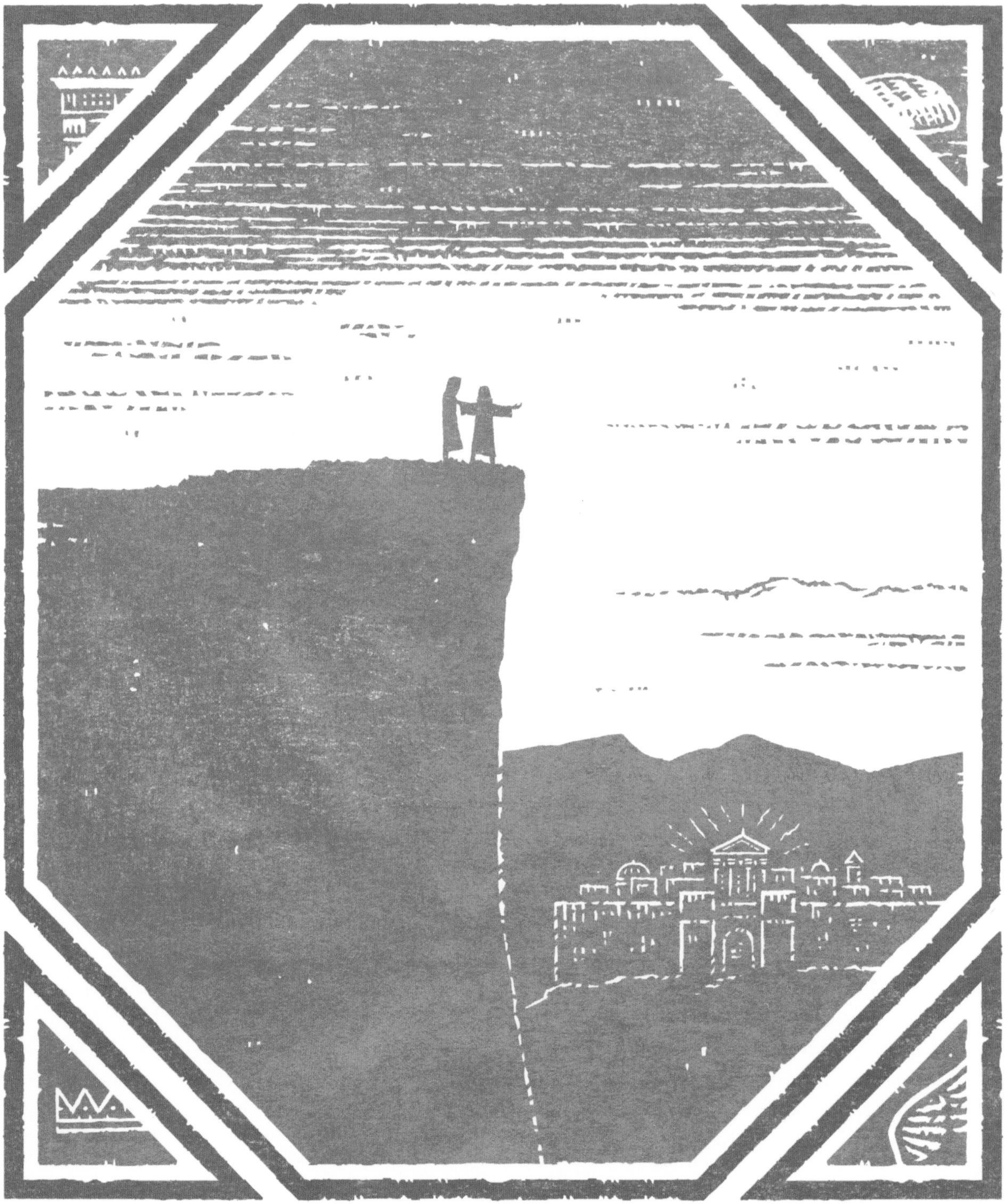

LITURGY FOR LENT

For the season of Lent, I have included readings for the first five Sundays of Lent. A separate liturgy for Palm Sunday and Holy Week is included in the following chapter. If you began reading a Gospel during Epiphany, continue that reading into Lent. These weeks leading up to Easter are ideal for meditating on the life of Christ.

Before you begin, light a candle (or the appropriate candles on your Lenten candle cross) and open your Bible to the week's reading. The words in **bold** are intended for everyone to say together as they are able.

Opening

"If anyone would come after me, let him deny himself and take up his cross and follow me" (Mark 8:34).

Antiphon

The Lord is full of compassion and mercy:
O come, let us adore him.

On the Feast of the Annunciation, use this instead:
The Word was made flesh and dwelt among us:
O come, let us adore him.

Prayer of Confession

You may alternately or additionally pray the Decalogue (page 125). Kneel as you are able.
Almighty and most merciful Father;
We have erred and strayed from your ways like lost sheep.
We have followed too much the devices and desires of our own hearts.
We have offended against your holy laws.
We have left undone those things which we ought to have done, and we have done
those things which we ought not to have done;
and apart from your grace, there is no health in us.
O Lord, have mercy upon us.
Spare all those who confess their faults.

Restore all those who are penitent, according to your promises declared to all people in Christ Jesus our Lord.

And grant, O most merciful Father, for his sake, that we may now live a godly, righteous, and sober life, to the glory of your holy Name. Amen.

Grant to your faithful people, merciful Lord, pardon and peace; that we may be cleansed from all our sins, and serve you with a quiet mind; through Jesus Christ our Lord. Amen.[12]

Scripture Reading

Anyone may do the reading. Once the reading has finished, perhaps take a minute to discuss and reflect on it together.

Ash Wednesday—Joel 2:1-2,12-17; Psalm 51

First Sunday in Lent—Deuteronomy 8:1-6,11-20; Matthew 4:1-11

Second Sunday in Lent—Exodus 17:1-7; John 4:5-42

Third Sunday in Lent—Exodus 16:4-18; John 6:1-15

Fourth Sunday in Lent—Exodus 20:1-21; Matthew 22:34-40

Fifth Sunday in Lent—Jeremiah 31:31-34; John 3:1-16

Sing Together

"Guide Me, O Thou Great Jehovah"

Pray

Take this time to pray as a family, lifting up your own needs and the needs of your community.

Lord's Prayer

Closing Prayer

Almighty God, you alone can bring into order the unruly wills and affections of sinners: Grant your people grace to love what you command and desire what you promise; that, among the swift and varied changes of this world, our hearts may surely there be fixed where true joys are to be found; through Jesus Christ our Lord, who lives and reigns with you and the Holy Spirit, one God, now and for ever. Amen.[13]

The Decalogue

God spoke these words and said: I am the LORD your God. You shall have no other gods but me.
Lord, have mercy upon us, and incline our hearts to keep this law.

You shall not make for yourself any idol.
Lord, have mercy upon us, and incline our hearts to keep this law.

You shall not take the Name of the LORD your God in vain.
Lord, have mercy upon us, and incline our hearts to keep this law.

Remember the Sabbath day and keep it holy.
Lord, have mercy upon us, and incline our hearts to keep this law.

Honor your father and your mother.
Lord, have mercy upon us, and incline our hearts to keep this law.

You shall not murder.
Lord, have mercy upon us, and incline our hearts to keep this law.

You shall not commit adultery.
Lord, have mercy upon us, and incline our hearts to keep this law.

You shall not steal.
Lord, have mercy upon us, and incline our hearts to keep this law.

You shall not bear false witness against your neighbor.
Lord, have mercy upon us, and incline our hearts to keep this law.

You shall not covet.
Lord, have mercy upon us, and write all these, your laws, in our hearts, we beseech you.[14]

EXODUS 20:1-17; DEUTERONOMY 5:6-21

Holy Week and the Triduum

And so the time comes to let you go again
like Mary at her weeping station
like Peter in his running shameful cry
like Mary Magdalene's sad watchful eye
like the soldier's gasping epiphany
like Joseph gently laying your body down and
    releasing you
into the tomb the darkness the empty unknown.

We would rather hang on to you friend
and let Simon take the cross as you slip out of line
catch a taxicab out of town
and escape into your suburban green lawn hideaway
where we drop by for a Sunday cookout and a Bud.
The mosquitoes would hover around us like angels
    singing "holy, holy, holy"
      and smell our breath and sweat
and bite you and draw a blood drop
and we look at each other and we know now
as we hang our weeping heads
that nothing ever gets done in clinging comfort.

And so the time comes to let you go again
and let God do the divine metamorphosis
of every weeping, shameful, sad, gasping, gentle
    release
into the tomb of darkness where you meet us in
    emptiness
where when we let you go we let ourselves go also
as we fall into the earthy black of surrender
and wait, wait, wait for your next creation out of
    nothing
your unexpected goodness bleeding through
your resurrection of everything we released to you
even ourselves in our fear of you and your
    mysterious ways.

MICHAEL COFFEY, "PASSIONTIDE"

At a Glance

STARTS: Palm Sunday

ENDS: Holy Saturday (the day before Easter)

TYPE: Preparation

DISCIPLINE: Confession

NOTABLE DATES:
Palm Sunday
Maundy Thursday
Good Friday

KEY VERSE: "All we like sheep have gone astray; we have turned—every one—to his own way; and the LORD has laid on him the iniquity of us all" (Isaiah 53:6).

HYMN: "O Sacred Head, Now Wounded"

FRUIT OF THE SPIRIT: Love

Holy Week concludes the season of Lent. In a mere six days, we manage to whiplash between the high-highs of Palm Sunday and the low-lows of Good Friday. To shepherd us through this rollercoaster of feeling and experience, the church has developed a special set of themes and services to draw us near to the Lord and prepare our hearts to celebrate the resurrection. Holy Week includes:

Passion or Palm Sunday (sixth Sunday of Lent)

Holy Monday, Tuesday, and Wednesday (sometimes known as "Spy" Wednesday)

Maundy Thursday

Good Friday

Holy Saturday

The period of time extending from the evening of Maundy Thursday through the evening of Easter Sunday is called the Paschal Triduum (trid-oo-um). *Triduum* is Latin for "three days," and these days are considered to be the very center of the church year. As it developed, the structure of the liturgy for the Holy Triduum was designed to communicate a single, continuous act of God. Emotionally, the disciples surely experienced the events from the Last Supper to the resurrection as one impossibly long day. The early church sought to replicate this experience with their forty-hour fast and various services of remembrance.

History

Once Christianity became legal in the Roman Empire in AD 313, Holy Week traditions developed in earnest, and the devout began to pilgrimage to the holy city for the Easter celebration. One such pilgrim was Egeria (or Aetheria), a nun from Spain. She visited Jerusalem in AD 395 and left detailed journal entries on the customs and events enjoyed during Holy Week. Like many pilgrims, she also brought these customs home, adapting them for the local church. While the church's current Holy Week liturgy has developed over time, its essential structure remains remarkably similar to Egeria's experiences.

Holy Week Places Us in God's Story

Holy Week not only places us in God's story but draws us, finally, to the very heart of the gospel. All of Scripture and the church's life and liturgy are developed around one theme: the crucifixion and resurrection of Christ and his attendant triumph over sin and death.

Throughout the Old Testament, the themes of Christ's death and resurrection are foreshadowed in several archetype tales, but none quite as powerful as the story of Passover. Indeed, the entire Triduum is commonly known as the Paschal (Passover) Triduum. When we fix our eyes on the cross, we see what John the Baptist proclaimed: "Behold the Lamb of

God, who takes away the sin of the world!" (John 1:29). As the blood of the spotless lamb in the Exodus story allowed God's wrath to pass over the Israelites, so Christ's blood also delivers us. And just as God pushed back the deep and deadly waters of the Red Sea, allowing his people to pass over from slavery to freedom, so Christ parted the grave to liberate us from the bondage of sin and death, granting us passage to eternal life with God.

It is imperative to understand the *passion* of Maundy Thursday, Good Friday, and Holy Saturday and the *passage* celebrated on Easter Sunday as one continuous act of God. When Christ declares from the cross, "It is finished," we witness God's great and terrible *kairos* as the power of sin and death are broken and resurrection becomes inevitable. As we—Christ's body—experience the Paschal Triduum, we consider afresh the way our own sin required Christ's passion, and we celebrate anew that we may follow Christ's passage from death to life.

Holy Week Is a Spiritual Discipline

As we move into Holy Week, we cannot help but be increasingly aware of the ways our sin required Jesus's death and of Christ's call for us to take up our own crosses and follow him. One way we do this is in the ancient discipline of *confession*. Julia Gatta and Martin L. Smith write, "The costly self-exposure we undergo in confession means we participate in the costliness of the cross."[1] The good news is that confession is also a discipline whereby we experience Christ's resurrection life.

> "Therefore, confess your sins to one another and pray for one another, that you may be healed." JAMES 5:16

The cycle of confession and forgiveness is constant in the life of the maturing Christian. It is the way by which we pursue holiness. As the Lord in his mercy brings conviction for our sins, we confess them, pray for forgiveness, and ask the Holy Spirit to enable us to walk evermore in newness of life. This cycle of confession has long been considered a renewal of our baptism[2]—just as in baptism we die to self and rise again in the life of Christ, so in confession we experience both death to self and resurrection life.

CONFESSION FAQS

Do I have to?

No. The old Anglican adage regarding confession is "All may. Some should. None must." But if you're shrinking from the idea of confession, I encourage you to examine why. If it's fear or shame, maybe confession is exactly what you need.

Can't I just confess my sins privately to the Lord?

Yes. You can. But remember, sin wants to stay hidden away in the dark. While a confession between you and the Lord is acceptable, there is less danger of self-deception and repeated offense when you bring your sin to the light before others. Bonhoeffer highlights the importance of confession within the context of a Christian community: "A man who confesses his sins in the presence of a brother knows that he is no longer alone with himself; he experiences the presence of God in the reality of the other person."[3]

To whom should I confess?

You could consider asking a pastor, trusted mentor, spiritual director, or friend to act as confessor. Your local Roman Catholic church almost certainly offers anonymous confession if anonymity is important to you. Choose someone who regularly practices confession themselves. Whoever you talk to should be adequately prepared ahead of time so it's not an awkward or uncomfortable experience for either of you.

Are the contents of my confession confidential?

Absolutely yes. If for some reason you find out that your confessor has betrayed your confidence, it's time to find a new confessor (unless you confessed to committing certain crimes, in which case confessors are both morally and legally obligated to report the offense to the authorities).

Will I be required to do penance?

Not in the Protestant tradition. Your confessor may—at the Holy Spirit's prompting—offer you a word of wisdom or some scriptural guidance for meditation and encouragement. But there is nothing *you* can do to atone for your sins; Jesus has already done that.

What does the time of confession actually entail?

There is no universal confession experience. Generally, the confession should be both as brief and as thorough as it needs to be. It should not include names, make excuses, or explain the backstory or extenuating circumstances.

Holy Week Is Communal

Once Christianity became legal in the Roman Empire, the days of Holy Week were publicly dedicated to activities of personal devotion. No secular work was done, and no entertainment was permitted. Monday through Wednesday were spent thoroughly cleaning the entire house (this may have been a holdover from the Jewish tradition of ritually cleansing a home before Passover). After cleaning, families would decorate for Easter by bringing green plants inside and making paper flowers. Everything was made sparkling for the coming Paschal Feast. On Thursday morning, bodies were cleaned (so if you haven't had your semiannual shower by Maundy Thursday, get it done!). Then Thursday evening, Friday, and Sunday were spent at church. Saturday was for food prep.

More than any other season, this is the week to prioritize being with the body of Christ. Remember that the church is wherever God's people gather, and this is *the week* to gather. If you are unable to attend services, clear space to observe the significance of each day with your family and in prayer.

Plan for Holy Week the way you plan for Christmas. On Monday through Wednesday, finish your meal planning and shopping for Maundy Thursday through Easter Monday so you don't have to think about those things during the Triduum. Prep your Easter clothes for Sunday. Also, Monday through Wednesday of Holy Week is a great time for spring cleaning! Divide your house into three zones and clean one per day. As part of the Lenten discipline of giving, clean out clothes and toys and donate items you don't need.

Palm Sunday

Palm Sunday kicks off Holy Week. It is the day the church gathers to remember Jesus's triumphal entry into Jerusalem. In many churches, congregants assemble outside the building, holding and waving palm branches and shouting, "Hosanna! Blessed is he who comes in the name of the Lord!" Singing together, everyone processes into the church to begin the service.

Remembering Palm Sunday

The best way to observe Palm Sunday is to go to church. Because of its physical and tactile elements, Palm Sunday is an especially beloved worship experience for children. Who doesn't love the opportunity to wave a big stick around and make a lot of noise? Once you're finished with your palms, take them home and put them in a vase for display.

If your church doesn't process or you can't make it to church, have your own procession at home. Either gather branches from your yard or make your own "palms" from green construction paper. Process through your yard or house shouting "Hosanna!"—and don't forget to read the story of Christ's triumphal entry either from Scripture or from a storybook Bible.

If your family is out of the phase of life where a homemade procession is spiritually beneficial, perhaps just purchase some palm leaves to place on your dining table and read the biblical narrative of Palm Sunday aloud together.

Holy Monday

On Holy Monday we remember when Mary (the sister of Lazarus) anointed Jesus's feet at Bethany. Taking perfumed oil worth a year's wages, Mary poured it on Jesus's feet and wiped his feet with her hair. In this act of love, humility, and honor we see, once again, the woman who has chosen "the good portion" (Luke 10:42). Judas was appalled by the "waste"—think of the good that could have been done with that money!—but Jesus rebuked him. In this moment of lavishness, Jesus affirmed Mary's instincts for loving worship.

Remembering Holy Monday

While there are no specific traditions related to this story, it is a good day for reflecting on what you offer to Jesus. Have you surrendered your whole life, all that you have and all that you are, or only part of it? If you're keeping something for yourself, why? Are you afraid, ashamed, angry, anxious? Take a few minutes to reflect on these questions, what your Lenten disciplines have taught you

about yourself, and the ways the Lord has been revealed to you through this season.

Holy Tuesday

On Holy Tuesday, Jesus entered Jerusalem and headed to the temple. Once there, he saw those who were profiting from worship, changing money, selling goods, and profaning God's holy place of worship. Jesus overturned the tables. He drove out the unrighteous. He cleansed the temple. But then he *stayed*, spending the next several days in the temple healing and teaching. In doing so, he restored the temple so that it could be used for its intended purpose: as a place for the people to meet with God, learn about him, and worship him.

Sometimes Jesus does this in our own lives as well—overturning the tables of our hearts to drive out our greed and opportunism, our misdirected loves and desires. And in doing so, he makes room for himself, a space where he can teach us and heal us.

Remembering Holy Tuesday

Make space in your home today. Even if you cannot spend Monday through Wednesday scrubbing the place from top to bottom, take Holy Tuesday to clean the unused, unnecessary, or unwanted items out of your home just as Jesus cleared the nonessential elements out of the temple.

Holy (or Spy) Wednesday

Holy Wednesday is sometimes called "Spy Wednesday" because it's the day we remember Judas's betrayal of Jesus for thirty pieces of silver.

Remembering Spy Wednesday

On Monday, Mary's story invites us to consider how much we love the Lord, and on Wednesday, Judas's betrayal prompts us to assess our allegiances. At what price do we value Jesus's life? Would we give him up for power? For love? For family? For money? If so, confess these things to the Lord and ask for forgiveness.

If you have younger children, gather 30 pieces of silver (quarters) and read the story of Judas betraying Jesus. Discuss the dangers of loving money more than God, and how God calls us to be generous with our resources (2 Corinthians 9:6-8). Add the "silver" to your Almsgiving Jar or simply put the money aside so your kids can add it to the offering plate on Sunday.

> "Christ our passover is sacrificed for us: Therefore let us
> keep the feast." 1 Corinthians 5:7-8 kjv

The Holy Triduum and Maundy Thursday

The word *maundy* comes from the Latin *mandatum*, meaning "commandment." After he finished washing their feet, Jesus told them, "A new commandment I give to you, that you love one another: just as I have loved you, you also are to love one another. By this all people will know that you are my disciples, if you have love for one another" (John 13:34-35). While these words are often read in the context of the foot washing, they ought also to be read in the context of Jesus's next actions: he submits to scourging, humiliation, rejection, torture, and an excruciating death because of his great love for us.

From the foot-washing narrative the story shifts to the Last Supper and the institution of the sacrament of the Lord's Table. There is a clear parallel to the Passover story as Christ tells his disciples they must consume his flesh, like the flesh of the Passover lamb, and drink his blood, the blood that delivers from God's wrath. Each time we partake of the Lord's Supper, we celebrate the new and better Passover—making present Christ's once-and-for-all sacrifice.

As we make present the events of Maundy Thursday, we experience Christ's loving care as he washes us clean and feeds us with the spiritual food of his most precious body and blood,[4] and yet we walk away from the evening with a knot of dread in our stomachs, knowing that the events of Good Friday are, in part, because of our failures. But while remembering the literal events and their spiritual implications for our own lives, we also share in God's final perspective, understanding these moments with the blessed relief of those who have a guaranteed seat at the wedding feast of the Lamb. With these shortcomings, sorrows, and hopes, we slip into Good Friday.

Remembering Maundy Thursday

If possible, go to a church service, have your feet washed, wash someone else's feet, receive Communion, and go in peace.

Foot Washing

If you cannot make it to church, grab a basin, a washcloth, and a few towels and set up a foot-washing station at home. Let each person take a turn having their feet washed and then washing someone else. Read the story of Christ's love in the upper room together, either from Scripture or a storybook Bible.

Last Supper

Another meaningful tradition families can practice is hosting a "Last Supper." This is not a Jewish Passover dinner and has a distinct liturgy and set of readings. Passover is still the most sacred holy day for the Jewish people, and Christians appropriating this meal to get in touch with their Jewish roots is profoundly offensive. In the same way we would not invite our neighbors from other religious traditions to partake in Communion, Christians should not be celebrating a Passover Seder unless, of course, invited by a Jewish neighbor to participate in *their* holiday meal.

That being said, a Last Supper does borrow from Seder traditions. Just as Christ's death and resurrection is a Passover story, so a Last Supper reinterprets Jewish Passover themes in light of Christ's finished work on the cross. For my own family, this meal has set the tone for the Triduum, helping my children enter into these days with sobriety, context, and comprehension of what we remember on Good Friday, mourn on Holy Saturday, and celebrate on Easter Sunday.

PRAYER VIGILS

Prayer vigils are customary on Maundy Thursday and Good Friday. These vigils allow congregants to stand in for the disciples in the Garden of Gethsemane that we may be present with Jesus in his anguish, keeping watch with him in prayer so that we "may not enter into temptation" (Luke 22:40). If your church doesn't offer a prayer vigil, consider organizing one.

> The dripping blood our only drink,
> The bloody flesh our only food:
> In spite of which we like to think
> That we are sound, substantial flesh and blood—
> Again, in spite of that, we call this Friday good.

T.S. Eliot, "East Coker IV," from *Four Quartets*

Good Friday

The term *Good* Friday is perhaps an indication that it was once called "God's Friday" in much the same way that *goodbye* is a truncated version of "God be with ye." But it is also, perhaps, an indication of how the church interprets the events of Friday rewording in comment. While the crucifixion is hardly "good" in the colloquial sense, when paired with the resurrection, it is in fact the very best thing that has ever happened in all of human history.

Liturgically, Good Friday is designed to be a time of mourning, prayer, and repentance as we, collectively and individually, reflect on how our own sin demanded the crucifixion. As he hangs on the cross, Christ allows the sins of all of humanity in all space and time to converge upon him as he gently, lovingly, agonizingly pours himself out in order to destroy its deadly power. We look on helpless, both grateful and horrified, as we witness this *kairos*.

The church services in which we contemplate our culpability in this painful scene are usually dark and somber. Traditionally, there is a fast from musical instruments (sometimes referred to as the Fast of the Ears). Communion is offered to those who wish to partake. There is no dismissal from this service. Once the priest says the final prayer of the Good Friday liturgy, he leaves, and the congregation is free to do the same. The service continues at the Great Vigil of Easter on Saturday evening.

Remembering Good Friday

I know I sound like a broken record in this chapter but...go to church! If you can, take Good Friday off from work.

Fasting

As with Ash Wednesday, it is customary to abstain from food on Good Friday, regardless of your chosen Lenten fast.[5] Some choose to fast from sundown on Maundy Thursday to sundown Good Friday. Some choose to fast starting at 3:00 p.m. Friday and don't break their fast until they take Communion at the Easter Vigil (Saturday evening) or at an Easter morning service. (There is something incredibly profound about taking the Eucharist when you are *very* hungry—it's a deeply physical reminder to feed on Jesus.)

STATIONS OF THE CROSS

The Stations of the Cross provide a guided meditation on Jesus's journey from Gethsemane to tomb. The fourteen stations are usually memorialized visually or sometimes with a tactile element kids can collect to help them recall the story. Individuals or families can also do the stations at home with your own set of art and readings.

Before each station, pray this prayer:

> We adore you, O Christ, and we bless you
> **By your holy cross, you have redeemed the world.**

Read the passage assigned to the station. After each reading, pray this:

> **Lord Jesus, have mercy on us, and help us to walk in your footsteps.**

Spend as much or as little time as you'd like in quiet contemplation before moving on to the next station.

1.	Jesus in the Garden of Gethsemane	Matthew 26:36-41
2.	Jesus is betrayed by Judas and arrested	Mark 14:43-46
3.	Jesus is condemned by the Sanhedrin	Luke 22:66-71
4.	Jesus is denied by Saint Peter	Matthew 26:69-75
5.	Jesus is judged by Pontius Pilate	Mark 15:1-5, 15
6.	Jesus is scourged at the pillar and crowned with thorns	John 19:1-3
7.	Jesus bears the cross	John 19:6, 15-17
8.	Jesus is helped by Simon the Cyrene to carry the cross	Mark 15:21
9.	Jesus meets the women of Jerusalem	Luke 23:27-31
10.	Jesus is crucified	Luke 23:33-34
11.	Jesus promises his kingdom to the repentant thief	Luke 23:39-43
12.	Jesus speaks to his mother and John	John 19:25-27
13.	Jesus dies on the cross	Luke 23:44-46
14.	Jesus is placed in the tomb	Matthew 27:57-60

Concluding Prayer

Almighty God, whose most dear Son went not up to joy but first he suffered pain, and entered not into glory before he was crucified: Mercifully grant that we, walking in the way of the cross, may find it none other than the way of life and peace; through Jesus Christ our Lord, who lives and reigns with you and the Holy Spirit, one God, forever and ever. Amen.[6]

HOT CROSS BUNS

Hot cross buns have been a Good Friday tradition since at least the fourteenth century, when a monk at Saint Albans Abbey in England baked rolls topped with a cross to distribute to the poor. However, the sweet buns may have originated significantly earlier as a treat to mark the end of the Lenten season. Like the Christmas puddings of yore, many of the ingredients of hot cross buns are symbolic—the spices representing the embalming spices used to prepare Christ's body, the bitter orange zest signifying the bitterness of the cross, and, of course, the cross on top symbolizing Christ's death.

Servings: 12

INGREDIENTS

Buns:
4½ cups bread flour (or all-purpose)
½ cup powdered sugar
1 T. instant or rapid-rise yeast
2 tsp. cinnamon powder
2 tsp. allspice
½ tsp. salt
1½ cups milk, warm
3½ T. unsalted butter, melted and cooled
1 egg
1½ cups white raisins
Zest of 1 or 2 oranges

Crosses:
½ cup flour
¼ cup water

Glaze:
1 T. apricot jam
2 tsp. water

DIRECTIONS

1. In the bowl of a stand mixer, combine 4¼ cups of flour with the sugar, yeast, cinnamon, allspice, and salt. Briefly mix with a dough hook.

2. Add the milk, butter, egg, raisins, and zest and mix on low speed until a smooth, elastic dough forms, approximately 5 minutes. After 1 minute, add up to ¼ cup of extra flour if required, just enough so the dough comes away from the side of the bowl when mixing and doesn't stick terribly to your fingers. (Alternatively, dust a work surface with flour and knead by hand for 10 minutes. Dough is kneaded enough when it's smooth and does not break when stretched.)

3. Leave the dough in the bowl, cover the bowl with plastic wrap, and place it in a warm place to rise until doubled in size, about 30 to 90 minutes.

4. Line a large baking sheet or a 9 x 13-inch pan with parchment paper with overhang.

5. Remove the plastic wrap and punch the dough to deflate.

6. Dust the work surface with flour, place the dough on the work surface, and shape it into a log. Cut the dough log into 12 equal pieces.

7. Take one piece of the dough and press it down with your palm, then use your fingers to gather and roll the dough briefly to form a ball. This stretches the dough on one side, which is how you get a nice smooth surface.

8. Place the ball on the baking sheet with the smooth side up. Repeat with the remaining dough, evenly spacing the 12 balls.

9. Spray a piece of plastic wrap lightly with oil, then loosely place it over the tray. Return the tray to a warm place and leave it for 30 to 45 minutes, or until the dough has risen by about 75 percent (less than double in size).

10. During the second rise, preheat the oven to 350°F.

11. Make the crosses: Mix the flour and water to make a thick, runny paste. Spoon the paste into a small ziplock bag, then snip the corner (just a little! You want a small hole). Remove the plastic wrap and use the paste to pipe crosses onto the buns. Go slowly so each cross hugs the curves of the roll.

12. Bake for 22 minutes, or until the surface is a deep golden brown. The surface color is the best test for doneness in this recipe.

13. Meanwhile, place the jam and water in a bowl, microwave it for 30 seconds, and stir it to combine.

14. When the buns are done, remove them from the oven. Use the overhang of parchment paper to lift the buns off the baking sheet and onto a cooling rack.

15. Brush the jam mixture over the buns while they are still hot. Allow the buns to cool to warm before serving.

Adapted with gratitude from Recipe Tin Eats

Holy Saturday

Following the intensity of Maundy Thursday and Good Friday, Holy Saturday can be completely disorienting. Whether we like it or not, Holy Saturday is the Sabbath. And as with any other Sabbath, we must rest from our work and have faith that God continues in his.

Holy Saturday teaches us something about grief that is simple and obvious, yet profoundly important: You have to go through it. Consider this: Once Jesus had breathed his last and God's purpose had been fulfilled, Jesus could have opened his eyes and popped off the cross (surprise!). Or he could have been entombed but risen Saturday morning. Instead, God honors sacred time and makes space for the Sabbath in the middle of his ultimate redeeming work. Even though God has something so very good to share, he allows space for his people to be ready to receive it.

As we consider the Paschal Triduum as one continuous act of God, let us not overlook that *rest* is an essential part of this act. As we consider the pain points of our own lives, our sorrows and griefs, let us not ignore the significance of our own Holy Saturdays. God's work may not be obvious to you in these moments, but he is most assuredly there, readying you to receive resurrection joy.

Observing Holy Saturday

Holy Saturday is also known as the Great Sabbath and has traditionally been a day for quiet preparation. Since the earlier parts of the week were spent preparing the home, the body, and the heart for Easter, Saturday was for preparing the food.

THE GREAT VIGIL OF EASTER

The Easter Vigil is a tradition nearly as old as Easter itself. After sundown (and often close to midnight or in the wee hours of the morning before sunrise), believers gather to celebrate the light of Christ, to rehearse the great story of God, to baptize those who have been prepared, and to feast—first on the Eucharist and then on the magnificent food prepared for Easter. This service bridges the themes of Lent and Easter, moving congregants from darkness to light and closing with a glorious celebration of the risen Lord.

If you can attend an Easter Vigil on Easter Eve, do so. It's a truly extraordinary service.

LITURGY FOR HOLY WEEK

For Holy Week, I have included the traditional daily readings that follow the story of Christ's last days. Before you begin, light a candle (or the appropriate candle on your Lenten candle cross) and open your Bible to the week's reading. Do not light any candles after Maundy Thursday. The words in **bold** are intended for everyone to say together as they are able.

Opening

"All we like sheep have gone astray; we have turned—every one—to his own way; and the LORD has laid on him the iniquity of us all" (Isaiah 53:6).

Antiphon

The Lord is full of compassion and mercy:
O come, let us adore him.

Prayer of Confession

Kneel as you are able.

Most merciful God, we confess that we have sinned against you in thought, word, and deed, by what we have done, and by what we have left undone.

We have not loved you with our whole heart; we have not loved our neighbors as ourselves.

We are truly sorry and we humbly repent.

For the sake of your Son Jesus Christ, have mercy on us and forgive us; that we may delight in your will, and walk in your ways, to the glory of your Name. Amen.[7]

Say or sing the Trisagion:
Holy God,
Holy and Mighty,
Holy Immortal One,
Have mercy on us.

Grant to your faithful people, merciful Lord, pardon and peace; that we may be cleansed from all our sins, and serve you with a quiet mind; through Jesus Christ our Lord. **Amen.**

Scripture Reading

Anyone may do the reading. Once the reading has finished, perhaps take a minute to discuss and reflect on it together.

> Palm Sunday—Mark 11:1-11
>
> Holy Monday—John 12:1-8
>
> Holy Tuesday—Mark 11:15-19
>
> Holy Wednesday—Matthew 26:1-5, 14-25
>
> Maundy Thursday—John 13:1-15; Luke 22:14-30
>
> Good Friday—John 18–19:37
>
> Holy Saturday—Matthew 27:57-66

Sing Together

"O Sacred Head, Now Wounded"

Pray

Take this time to pray as a family, lifting up your own needs and the needs of your community.

Lord's Prayer

Closing Prayer

Assist us mercifully with your grace, Lord God of our salvation, that we may enter with joy upon the meditation of those mighty acts by which you have promised us life and immortality; through Jesus Christ our Lord, who lives and reigns with you and the Holy Spirit, one God, for ever and ever. Amen.[8]

EASTER

Expect the end of the world. Laugh.
Laughter is immeasurable. Be joyful
though you have considered all the facts....
Practice resurrection.

Wendell Berry
"Manifesto: The Mad Farmer Liberation Front"

STARTS: Easter Sunday

ENDS: Feast of Pentecost

TYPE: Celebration

DISCIPLINE: Sabbath

NOTABLE DATES:
Easter Sunday
Rogationtide
Feast of the Ascension
Pentecost

KEY VERSE: "If then you have been raised with Christ, seek the things that are above, where Christ is, seated at the right hand of God" (Colossians 3:1).

HYMN: "Christ the Lord Is Risen Today"

FRUIT OF THE SPIRIT: Joy

Alleluia! The Lord is risen! (*The Lord is risen indeed! Alleluia!*) Contrary to how it's popularly celebrated, Easter is not a one-off celebration, but the inauguration of the Great Fifty Days of Easter. Just as Christmas Day is the opening of the Feast of Christmas, Easter Sunday is an overture of the coming season rather than the grand finale of Lent. Eastertide (also called Paschaltide) is fifty full days stretching from the First Sunday of Easter (commonly just called Easter) until the eighth Sunday of Easter (the Feast of Pentecost). These fifty days are *all* Easter—one long, continuous celebration of the resurrection. Just as we set aside one-seventh of our week as holy unto the Lord, we set aside the season of Easter—approximately one-seventh of our year—as consecrated time.

History

From the earliest days of the church, Christians have gathered each Sunday to worship and celebrate the death and resurrection of Christ. Easter remains the church's oldest yearly celebration and the feast around which all other liturgical calendar traditions are built.

At the council of Nicaea in AD 325, the Easter celebration was "fixed" on the first Sunday after the first full moon following the vernal (spring) equinox on March 21. If this seems strangely complicated, that's because it is. The council sought to maintain the calendrical link between Easter and Passover, but the Jewish religious year is based on the lunar cycle. Passover was to take place in the seventh month (Nisan) as measured by full moon cycles. So when the date of Easter was "fixed," it was done according to the Jewish calendar. Easter is often, though not always, the Sunday after Passover.[1]

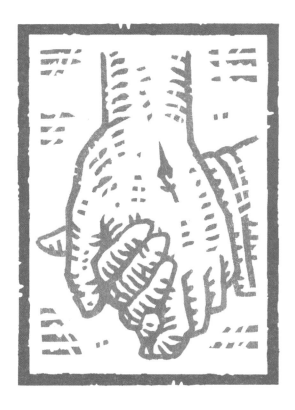

Easter Places Us in God's Story

When Christ walks out of the tomb, his ignominious death is revealed to be the ark of salvation; the dead wood of the cross becomes a tree that bears fruit; and those who were dead to sin become new creations in Christ.

Containing seven Sundays, forty-nine days, Easter is celebrated as a "Week of Weeks." In the Bible, seven is considered the number of fullness or completion, which is fitting because, as Laurence Stookey notes, "Christ is fullness heaped upon fullness, and so can be symbolized by seven times seven."[2] You may note, however, that Eastertide actually has eight Sundays, not seven. While we celebrate Christ's fullness as symbolized in the "week of weeks," we also celebrate Christ's inauguration of the new creation with an eighth Sunday as the final and full redemption of all things.[3]

Though the season finds its completion in eight Sundays, the whole of Eastertide is considered the final movement of the Holy Triduum. It's what Bobby Gross describes as "both culmination and inauguration."[4] Easter is simultaneously what all of creation has been waiting for since the fall—a reconciliation between maker and made—*and* the dawn of an extraordinary new reality. No longer are we bound by sin and death, but risen with Christ in glory, united with him by his Holy Spirit. Theologian N.T. Wright explains, "Jesus's resurrection is the beginning of God's new project not to snatch people away from earth to heaven but to colonize earth with the life of heaven."[5] Easter calls us not only to a contemplation of Christ's resurrection—his literal rising from the dead—but also to the way his life is manifest in us now and to our own bodily resurrection in the final restoration of all creation.

Easter Is a Spiritual Discipline

For both Jews and Christians, consecrating one day of the week as holy unto the Lord has always been central to faith and practice. For the Jews—including Jesus—it was the Sabbath.

A lot can be gleaned from the Jewish tradition of Sabbath. It is a time of worship, fellowship, feasting, rest, and ultimately restoration and refreshment—it sounds a lot like Luke's description of the church in Acts 2:42! Sabbath is an offering of our time, consecrated for the purpose of finding refreshment through obedience to God's commands. Practicing Sabbath well is an act of faith, an affirmation that six days of work with God are better than seven days of work without him.

As you enter into the season of Easter, consider how you can honor sacred time each week.

Easter Is Communal

So you made it through the wilderness of Lent to the glorious promised land of Easter! Now what? As H. Boone Porter writes, "It's a strange irony that many church people try to live faithfully during Lent to observe forty days of preparation, yet virtually abandon Eastertide after going to church on Easter Day."[6] Everything we've done thus far in the liturgical year has its meaning because of the resurrection of Jesus Christ. Let's not forsake the feast now!

"Easter is about the wild delight of God's creative power.... We ought to shout Alleluias instead of murmuring them; we should light every candle in the building instead of only some; we should give every man, woman, child, cat, dog, and mouse in the place a candle to hold; we should have a real bonfire; we should splash water about as we renew our baptismal vows. Every step back from that is a step toward an ethereal or esoteric Easter experience, and the thing about Easter is that it is neither ethereal nor esoteric. It's about the real Jesus coming out of the real tomb and getting God's real new creation under way."

N.T. WRIGHT, *SURPRISED BY HOPE*

Obviously, fifty days of lavish Easter feasting is just not sustainable, so let's consider a few practical ways to orient our hearts to this season.

First, I encourage you to lean into your own spiritual growth. If Lent was a time for making space—for weeding and tilling the soil of your heart—then Easter is a time for planting seeds, watering them, and watching for what God will cultivate in you. Be intentional about what you plant in this season. Second, focus on making all eight Sundays of the Great Feast of Easter an extra celebratory occasion. Here are some options:

- Invite friends and family for a meal.
- Keep fresh flowers around your house as a reminder of new life.
- Prepare special meals or decadent desserts.
- Plant a garden.
- Have a bonfire night or light *lots* of candles.
- Host an Easter hymn sing.
- Enjoy local parks and playgrounds to relish the spring weather and "play" together as a family.
- Hold a rammalation biscuit baking contest on Rogation Sunday (pages 159-161).
- Enjoy a hilltop picnic for Ascension Sunday (pages 166-169).
- Throw a birthday party for the church on Pentecost (pages 170-173).
- Establish a Sabbath rhythm as a family.
- Above all, go to church and worship!

YOU'RE INVITED TO SABBATH!

Who

All Christians seeking to walk in repentance and faith

What

Take a Sabbath rest. In *Ten Words to Live By*, Jen Wilkin describes our over-eager work ethic as the "self-appointed slavery of self-gain."[7] We are to combat this self-inflicted oppression with God's rest. She writes: "Sabbath is the deliberate cessation of any activity that might reinforce my belief in my own self-sufficiency.... It requires that we deny ourselves the material gain or sense of accomplishment a day of labor brings."[8]

When

The day is your choice. Paul writes in Romans 14:5-6, "One person esteems one day as better than another, while another esteems all days alike.... The one who observes the day, observes it in honor of the Lord." If you are a person who cannot cease their labor on Sunday, choose another day to Sabbath. The concept of primary importance here is *how* you observe your Sabbath and not when.[9]

Regarding the *time*, try to observe your Sabbath from sundown to sundown. What better way to enter Sabbath rest than by going to sleep, waking to the resurrected sun, and finding God is already at work so that we may rest in peace?

How

Effectual Sabbath rest requires both praying and playing because, as Eugene Peterson observes, "Playing and praying counter boredom, reduce anxieties, push, pull, direct, prod us into the fullness of our humanity by getting body and spirit in touch and friendly with each other."[10]

Additionally, when we Sabbath, we stop our work so that others may stop their work as well. Jen Wilkin notes, "If someone else's work secures our rest, we are more than likely enjoying the rest of privilege, but not of Sabbath."[11]

TIPS FOR SABBATH KEEPING

And Jesus said to them, "The Sabbath was made for
man, not man for the Sabbath" (Mark 2:27).

- Remember that each Sunday is a feast. Consider some of the feasting suggestions on page 64 if you need some inspiration on ways to "pray and play" together on your Sabbath.

- Factor your Sabbath into your weekly plans. Perhaps try to organize your Sabbaths a month in advance—plan to host friends, go to a local park, or have a family movie night.

- Choose Sabbath activities that are life-giving for you and your family. For me, that sometimes means writing, home-improvement projects, or making an elaborate meal I don't have time for on a weekday (or a Crock-Pot meal so I don't have to think about cooking at all that day).

- Decide ahead of time what you will *not* do on the Sabbath—for me, it's laundry and answering work email.

- If you are a parent, especially of young children, you know that a true cessation from work feels like an impossibility. There are mini-humans to feed and diapers to change, spills to wipe up and faces to wipe off. Reframe your consideration of this work as tasks you *get* to do rather than work you *have* to do. God has blessed you with the joy and care of children. Just as he never ceases his care for us—even on the Sabbath—we never cease our care for them.

- Remember that sometimes Sabbathing well is hard, and you will fail at it. Let it go and try again next week.

The Sundays of Easter

Within the church, each Sunday in Easter has a specific theme, and the lectionary readings of these weeks have a twofold focus:

1. On the character of Jesus and his interactions with his disciples after the resurrection;

2. On the gospel going forth into the world via the early church in the book of Acts.

These readings culminate on Pentecost with the story of Jesus promising to send the Holy Spirit from John 14 and the descent of the Holy Spirit in Acts 2. Within this reading structure "is a sturdy affirmation that the church is built upon the resurrection and its proclamation by people of faith."[12]

- **First Sunday of Easter**—Easter Sunday: This day is focused on the literal events of Jesus's resurrection.

- **Second Sunday of Easter**—Thomas Sunday: On this day we remember Thomas's incredulity and how God gently meets us in our doubt.

- **Third Sunday of Easter**—Meal Sunday: Jesus spent forty days on earth after his resurrection, and much of this time was spent eating with his friends. After he met two of the apostles on the road to Emmaus, he "took the bread and blessed and broke it and gave it to them. And their eyes were opened.... He was known to them in the breaking of the bread" (Luke 24:30-35). With the clear parallel to the institution of the Lord's Supper in Luke 22, Jesus is showing us that the sacrament should not just be a simple reminder of his crucifixion but a celebratory feast of his resurrection wherein our eyes may be opened and we may be whole as well.

- **Fourth Sunday of Easter**—Good Shepherd Sunday: This week we read Psalm 23 and Jesus's "I am the Good Shepherd" passage. We remember his care and tenderness toward his sheep.

- **Fifth Sunday of Easter**—I AM Sunday: Any one of Jesus's "I am" statements found in the book of John can be the focus for this Sunday. These statements are ways Christ revealed himself as the great I AM of the burning bush, the Holy One of Israel in whom everything exists.

- **Sixth Sunday of Easter**—Rogation Sunday: This Sunday begins a four-day period of intercession known as Rogationtide (see page "Rogation Days" on page 159).

- **Seventh Sunday of Easter**—Ascension Sunday

- **Eighth Sunday of Easter**—Day of Pentecost

The latter two Sundays will be detailed on pages 165-173.

RESURRECTION ROLLS

These rolls are best made *with* your children so they can enjoy and understand the "resurrection" part of resurrection rolls. Together, on the eve of Easter, place the marshmallow in the crescent roll tomb. On Easter morning, bake the rolls and—viola! An empty tomb! And a delightful treat.

Yield: 8 rolls

INGREDIENTS

1 (12 oz.) package refrigerated crescent rolls
¼ cup sugar
1 T. ground cinnamon
8 large marshmallows
¼ cup butter, melted

DIRECTIONS

1. Separate the rolls into eight triangles. Combine the sugar and cinnamon. Dip each marshmallow into butter, roll it in the cinnamon-sugar mixture, and place it on a triangle. Pinch the dough around the marshmallow, sealing all edges. Make sure to seal it well or the marshmallow will escape.

2. Brush the tops of the dough with the remaining butter and sprinkle with the cinnamon-sugar mixture. Place each dough piece with the sugar side up in greased muffin cups.

3. Bake at 375°F for 10 to 15 minutes or until rolls are golden brown. Allow to cool slightly then eat warm.

Easter in Your Home

1. Alleluia banners. If you buried alleluia banners at the beginning of Lent, go dig them up and display them for the season of Easter. Just tape them to your wall—it doesn't have to be perfect, just joyful. If you didn't bury any banners, make or buy a new one and keep it up during Eastertide.

2. Feast of the Eyes. If you covered your cross or other religious art for Lent, uncover it!

3. Decorate. It's time to swap your Lenten decor for Easter decor—get rid of the violet and exchange it for white and gold linens or something else colorful and festive; get rid of the dry sticks and fill your space with fresh flowers; keep your candle cross and light all your candles as a celebration of the risen Light of the World.

And don't forget to keep your Easter decorations up for all fifty days!

Easter Traditions

From most sacred to least...

Greeting

On Easter, it is customary to greet your fellow saints with "The Lord is risen!" to which they respond, "He is risen indeed! Alleluia!"

Easter Lilies

These springtime beauties have long been used as Easter symbols for their pure white color and their trumpetlike shape alluding to an announcement of good news! Spring flowers are also beautiful symbols of resurrection life.

Blessing the Food

In many communities, it was tradition to prepare special food for Easter on Holy Saturday and take it to your local church to be blessed by a priest. These blessings were for the purpose of consecrating the familial Easter feasts as holy unto the Lord.

BLESSING FOR EASTER FOOD

Blessed are you, O Lord our God; you bring forth food from the earth and make the risen Lord to be for us the Bread of life: Grant that we who daily seek the food which sustains our bodies may also hunger for the food of everlasting life, Jesus Christ our Lord. Amen.[13]

A "Blessing over Wine" can be found on page 69.

PRO TIP: If you'd like to dye your own red eggs, you can easily do so with yellow onion skins! You will need skins from 10 to 15 onions, so I suggest starting to save your onion skins in a refrigerated bag at the beginning of Lent.

Eggs

Ah, the Easter egg. It is certainly one of the most recognizable, if not the most beloved, of all Easter symbols. Like flowers, eggs have ever been symbols of spring and new life, and the dyeing and exchange of eggs have their roots in Egyptian and Persian spring rituals. Unlike the bunny, however, eggs also have a long history of rich symbolism within church life.

The legend starts with Mary Magdalene—the first to hear of Jesus's resurrection from the angel, the first to see the resurrected Christ, and the first to share this good news with the other disciples. One legend goes that Mary brought cooked eggs to share with her fellow women when they went to anoint the body of Jesus. When she beheld the risen Christ, her eggs miraculously turned bright red!

Whether or not we believe the legend, the fact remains that exchanging red eggs on Easter is a longstanding tradition throughout Europe. The red dye represents the blood of Christ; the eggshell, the tomb. And when the eggshell is cracked open to reveal a brilliant white egg, we remember the cracking of the tomb and the emergence of a whole and triumphant Christ.

Practically speaking, though many fasted from eggs for Lent, no one managed to communicate this to the hens. So while most people were busy not consuming eggs, hens were still busy laying them. To protect this bounty from spoiling, eggs were dyed, cooked and saved for Easter.

WHAT ABOUT THE EASTER BUNNY?

German legend has it that a woman once hid Easter eggs in a nest. When her children discovered the eggs, a rabbit was seen hopping nearby, and they assumed it had laid the eggs. This myth eventually morphed into the German *Osterhase* (Easter Hare), which would bring treats and eggs to well-behaved children. German immigrants to America brought the tradition across the Atlantic, where Americans did as Americans do—used it to make money. All this to say, enjoy it as a fun tradition if you wish, but there's no particular biblical or historical church reason to incorporate the bunny into your Easter celebrations.

Easter Baskets

Nothing says "celebration" to a child like presents! My husband and I tell our children they receive gifts on Easter as a symbol of our gratitude for all that God has given us, especially the gift of salvation by the death and resurrection of Jesus. We usually fill their baskets with a few treats, a new bathing suit, chalk, bubbles, and a book to support their spiritual life. Scripture journals, prayer candles, icons, prayer beads, or other items to encourage their devotional life would be appropriate as well.

Easter Egg Hunt

There's no particular meaning to this tradition, though when my son was five, he excitedly explained to us how when we hunt for eggs, we're like the apostles running around looking for Jesus. It's as good a theological explanation for an egg hunt as any! If you'd like to add another theological layer to your egg hunt, pray this prayer of blessing and enjoy God's bounty.

BLESSING THE EGG HUNT

O Lord our God, in celebration of Easter we have prepared these eggs from your creation: Grant that they may be to us a sign of the resurrection life promised to those who follow your Son, our Lord Jesus Christ. As we place these blessed eggs in our baskets, may we always remember to carry your good news to the world. **Amen**.

Rogation Days

Rogation Days (or Rogationtide) is a quirky little season-within-a-season dedicated to intercession for the agricultural economy (though in recent years it's been expanded to include all economies). *Rogation* comes from the Latin *rogare,* "to ask."

It consists of four days starting on the fifth Sunday in Easter and ending the Wednesday before the Feast of the Ascension, which is always a Thursday.

This tradition dates back to AD 470 when several natural disasters ravaged Vienne, France. Bishop Mamertus of Vienne declared a period of prayer and fasting to petition the Lord for protection from earthquakes and other catastrophes, which could decimate both a region and its annual livelihood. Rogation Days were sensible to all, and the observance quickly spread throughout France, south into Italy, and north into England. It was added to the official church calendar by Pope Leo III in the late eighth century.

In England, Rogationtide was most notably marked by the "beating of the bounds." When people were assigned to churches based on a parish model,[14] priests would lead their congregations in a procession around the boundaries of their parish, praying for its protection in the coming year. At certain key boundary markers (extra-large trees, bodies of water, and the like), boys would be beaten with willow switches or chucked into said bodies of water—this would help the boys (and the parishioners at large) to remember *exactly* where their parish boundaries were. Hence, "beating" the boundaries. In later times, stone boundary markers would be beaten with branches, which seems...more humane. The English processions eventually became *very* elaborate and featured a number of symbolic banners, saint icons, large torches, and ganging beer.

No one is entirely sure *what* ganging beer was. Rogation Days were referred to by the English as "Gang Day" or "Gan Week," which comes from the Old English word for "walking" or "going." It's entirely possible that ganging beer is just beer they drank while "ganging" and there's no special recipe. The drink, however, is much less mysterious than the traditional "rammalation biscuit" eaten on the walk. For one thing, scholars have no idea what *rammalation* means. The best theory is that, like ganging beer, they were just the biscuits consumed during Rogationtide and there was no special recipe or deeper meaning.

This mini 'tide significantly shaped Christian thought and practice over time. Anglican priest and poet George Herbert writes of four reasons for Rogationtide:

- to seek God's blessing for fruitful fields,
- to seek the preservation of justice within the parish boundaries,
- to (literally) walk in love and reconcile differences with one another, and
- to use God's provision to practice mercy and generosity toward the poor.[15]

Despite the fact that most no longer live in an agricultural economy, these days have a lot to teach Christians about how we exist in the world, the way in which we interact with God's creation, and our eschatological views.

Rogationtide is an earthy call to remember that *all* creation will one day be exalted and the Lord will dwell here with us. The Lord promises to renew the face of the earth (Psalm 104:30), and its restoration begins with the dawn of the new creation on Easter morning. Since the Garden of Eden God has called man to care for the earth, and this task will continue to be ours into eternity.

Though many of us now work with our minds in cities rather than with our hands in fields, we recall that our labors are not in vain. Time began in a garden, but it ends in a city—the great heavenly city of God come down to earth (Revelation 21:2). God made us to work and to steward his creation, which includes the work of the mind and modern innovations of the information age. Rogationtide is an annual reminder of this holy task and the sanctification of our labor.

Prayer for Rogation Days

Almighty God, whose Son Jesus Christ in his earthly life shared our toil and hallowed our labor: Be present with your people where they work; make those who carry on the industries and commerce of this land responsive to your will; and give us all a right satisfaction in what we do, and a just return for our labor; through Jesus Christ our Lord, who lives and reigns with you, in the unity of the Holy Spirit, one God, now and forever. **Amen.**[16]

Observing Rogation Days

Prayer Walk

Walk and pray in your own neighborhood, around your children's schools, around your office building, or any other locale that is meaningful to you. If you want to focus on agriculture but live in an urban area, walk around your grocery store and surreptitiously pray for the farmers who grow and produce our food. Literally walk and pray if you can, but if you cannot, "walk and pray" in your mind. Take your children and walk with them, stopping to pray where appropriate. Pray for God's fruitfulness and protection over these significant spaces of your life and thank him for his provision.

Sing

"O Jesus Crowned with All Renown" was written for and is traditionally sung during Rogationtide

Bake-Off or Brew-Off

If you're looking for a fun Rogation Sunday feast activity, perhaps invite your fellow churchgoers to a rammalation biscuit baking contest. *Biscuit* can be pretty broadly defined as anything from that fluffy, buttery breakfast delight to a gingersnap cookie. Let everyone decide for themselves what *biscuit* means and get to baking!

Alternately, if you're lucky enough to know a handful of home brewers, challenge them to a brew-off and find out who can make the best keg of ganging beer.

LITURGY FOR EASTERTIDE

Before you begin, light a candle and open your Bible to the week's reading. The words in **bold** are intended for everyone to say together as they are able.

From Easter Day until the Feast of the Ascension:

Opening

"If then you have been raised with Christ, seek the things that are above, where Christ is, seated at the right hand of God" (Colossians 3:1).

Antiphon

Alleluia. The Lord is risen indeed:
O come, let us adore him. Alleluia.

From the Feast of the Ascension until Pentecost:

Opening

"Since then we have a great high priest who has passed through the heavens, Jesus, the Son of God, let us hold fast our confession.... Let us then with confidence draw near to the throne of grace, that we may receive mercy and find grace to help in time of need" (Hebrews 4:14, 16).

Antiphon

Alleluia. Christ the Lord has ascended into heaven:
O come, let us adore him. Alleluia.

Scripture Reading

Anyone may do the reading. Once the reading has finished, perhaps take a minute to discuss and reflect on it together.

First Sunday of Easter—Matthew 28:1-10; Acts 10:34-43

Second Sunday of Easter—John 20:19-31; Acts 5:12,17-29

Third Sunday of Easter—Luke 24:13-35; Acts 4:5-14

Fourth Sunday of Easter—John 10:11-16; Psalm 23

Fifth Sunday of Easter—John 14:1-14; Acts 8:26-40

Sixth Sunday of Easter—John 15:1-11; Acts 17:22-34

Feast of the Ascension—find a mini-liturgy for this day on page 169

Seventh Sunday of Easter—John 17:1-11; Acts 1:6-14

Eighth Sunday of Easter (the Day of Pentecost): a Pentecost liturgy is on page 173

Sing Together

"Christ the Lord Is Risen Today"

Pray

Take this time to pray as a family, lifting up your own needs and the needs of your community.

Lord's Prayer

Closing Prayer

O God, who by the glorious resurrection of your Son Jesus Christ destroyed death and brought life and immortality to light: Grant that we, who have been raised with him, may abide in his presence and rejoice in the hope of eternal glory; through Jesus Christ our Lord, to whom, with you and the Holy Spirit, be honor and glory, now and for ever. Amen.

ASCENSION AND PENTECOST

We saw his light break through the cloud of glory
Whilst we were rooted still in time and place
As earth became a part of Heaven's story
And heaven opened to his human face.
We saw him go and yet we were not parted
He took us with him to the heart of things
The heart that broke for all the broken-hearted
Is whole and Heaven-centred now, and sings,
Sings in the strength that rises out of weakness,
Sings through the clouds that veil him from our sight,
Whilst we our selves become his clouds of witness
And sing the waning darkness into light,
His light in us, and ours in him concealed,
Which all creation waits to see revealed.

MALCOLM GUITE, "THE ASCENSION"

ASCENSION

"He ascended into heaven and is seated at the right hand of the Father. He will come again in glory to judge the living and the dead."

THE APOSTLES' CREED

When it was determined that the season of Easter should be considered one continuous day, it was in large part because the work of the cross was vindicated not only in Christ's resurrection but also in his ascension and at Pentecost. These two holy days are theologically inseparable from the events of the Holy Triduum.

The Ascension

The Feast of the Ascension is one of the oldest, most important, and most overlooked holidays of the church year. According to Acts 1, Jesus ascended into heaven forty days after the resurrection: Jesus "was lifted up, and a cloud took him out of their sight" (Acts 1:9). Since the first century, it has been the day the church has remembered Christ ascending the throne in heaven and being seated at the right hand of the Father, with all authority on heaven and earth given to him and all things placed under his dominion (Ephesians 1:20-23).

This day "marks the completion of our Lord's redemptive work."[1] After breaking the power of sin and death with his risen body, Jesus—still fully human—is exalted to a place of heavenly headship. It is the completion of what we celebrate at Christmas, an inverse great exchange: Whereas at the incarnation we marvel that God debased himself by descending to earth and taking on human flesh, at the ascension we marvel that he glorifies human flesh by ascending in it to heaven. In doing so, Christ

1. confirms our own participation in his resurrection,
2. affirms the importance of the physical world and our work in it, and
3. reveals how we should live as we await his return, for if our bodies and our physical world are being redeemed, then what we do with our bodies in our physical world matters.

The question the ascension asks is, Do we live, work, play, and pray in this world as if we are its heirs, and as if we are stewarding the place that is becoming the kingdom of heaven?

Celebrating the Ascension

Because the Feast of the Ascension always happens on a Thursday, it is most often celebrated by the church on the following Sunday, which is the seventh Sunday in Easter.

Hike

Whether you celebrate on the feast day itself or on Sunday, most traditions include a walk or hike to a hilltop to commemorate Jesus leading his disciples out to Bethany and the Mount of Olives before he ascended (Luke 24:50).

Eat

Once on the hill, you picnic! In the Middle Ages, it was customary to eat birds on Ascension Day because Jesus "flew" into heaven (it's a tenuous link, to be sure). Perhaps pack a chicken salad for lunch. Bird-shaped pastries are also encouraged.

Celebrate

If you have children who love balloons, you may consider getting one helium balloon for each child and helping them draw either a picture of Jesus or write a prayer on their balloon, then go outside, release the balloons, and watch them ascend. You could also blow bubbles, fly kites, or release butterflies for a similar effect.

A NOTE ON BALLOON RELEASES

While this would be a memorable tradition for children, I do want to note that intentionally releasing balloons in this manner can be considered littering, which seems a *bit* antithetical to the whole creation-care point of the Feast of the Ascension. So if you want to release the balloons, please do it responsibly:

- Use biodegradable balloons.
- Don't use plastic discs to secure the balloon—just tie a knot.
- Take the strings or ribbons off the balloons before you release them.

LITURGY FOR ASCENSION

Antiphon

Alleluia! Christ the Lord has ascended into heaven.
O come, let us adore him. Alleluia!

Scripture Readings

Luke 24:50-53
Hebrews 4:14-16

Sing Together

"Crown Him with Many Crowns"

Pray

Almighty God, whose only-begotten Son our Lord Jesus Christ ascended into heaven: May our hearts and minds also there ascend, and with him continually dwell; who lives and reigns with you and the Holy Spirit, one God, for ever and ever. Amen.[2]

PENTECOST

Creator Spirit, by whose aid
Th' world's foundations first were laid,
Come, visit ev'ry pious mind;
Come, pour thy joys on human kind;
From sin, and sorrow set us free;
And make thy temples worthy Thee.

JOHN DRYDEN, "VENI, CREATOR SPIRITUS" ("COME, CREATOR SPIRIT")

Pentecost is both the beginning and the end of Eastertide as Sunday is both the first and eighth day of creation. Pentecost represents the completion of the work begun on the cross, manifest in the resurrection, and promised at the Ascension. On this Sunday, this eighth day of creation, what exactly did God create? The church! As Christ called forth a new creation by his resurrection, the church became his body.

As an official church feast, Pentecost has been celebrated since at least the third century. Pentecost is the finale of Easter, the capstone of the Holy Triduum, and the birthday of the church! It is the day we celebrate the fulfillment of God's promise to Joel, "I will pour out my spirit on all flesh" (Joel 2:28), the moment when "the Risen Christ is made present to the church."[3] In addition, Pentecost kicks off the season of Ordinary Time, which is also known as the time of the Holy Spirit or the time of the church.

After the Spirit descends in Acts 2, evangelism begins in earnest: "and the Lord added to their number day by day those who were being saved" (Acts 2:47). In this scene we see a parallel to and a reversal of the Tower of Babel.

170

WHAT'S IN A ~~NAME~~ NUMBER?

The word *Pentecost* literally means "fiftieth day." In the Bible, fifty is the number of restitution and liberation magnificently symbolized in the Year of Jubilee as commanded in Leviticus 25. Every seventh year, the Jews were to grant a Sabbath rest to their land—allowing it to lie fallow. And every seven Sabbath years—that is, after forty-nine years—they were to consecrate the fiftieth year as holy, a Sabbath of Sabbaths, a Year of Jubilee. During this time, there was not only a rest for the land but a rest for the people from debt, servitude, and bondage. Symbolically, Christ's resurrection is the great fiftieth year as it is also the eighth day of creation. Fifty days of Eastertide is a symbol of the freedom we have in Christ, and the beginning of a new creation no longer bound by the yoke of sin or the law (see Galatians 5:1).

On Pentecost, we celebrate the unity of the church as a community of the Spirit. By the Holy Spirit, the church is gifted with supernatural connectedness, an enduring commonality that breaks down cultural, socioeconomic, gender, language, ethnic, and (dare I say it?) denominational barriers. On the day of Pentecost and throughout the rest of the book of Acts, there is a stunning picture of what it looks like for a diverse church to be unified and for the unified church to be diverse.

This Pentecost miracle is a terrific annual reminder to be constantly orienting our hearts toward the unity of the church, pursuing wholeness with respect, kindness, and graciousness, being willing to converse, quick to forgive, and above all, loving toward our brothers and sisters with whom we find disagreement.

A PRAYER FOR THE UNITY OF ALL CHRISTIAN PEOPLE

O God the Father of our Lord Jesus Christ, our only Savior, the Prince of Peace: Give us grace to take to heart the grave dangers we are in through our many divisions. Deliver your church from all enmity and prejudice, and everything that hinders us from godly union. As there is one Body and one Spirit, one hope of our calling, one Lord, one Faith, one Baptism, one God and Father of us all, so make us all to be of one heart and of one mind, united in one holy bond of truth and peace, of faith and love, that with one voice we may give you praise; through Jesus Christ our Lord, who lives and reigns with you and the Holy Spirit, one God in everlasting glory. Amen.[4]

Celebrating Pentecost

Worship

In case I need to say it, go to church on Pentecost!

Decorate

Red roses have long been associated with the feast because their blooms look like tongues of flame. One old tradition that we should *absolutely* revive is that of scattering red rose petals (tongues of flame) on churchgoers as they enter their church building on the day of Pentecost.

Party

As far as birthday parties go, this one ought to be second only to Christ's. Churches should be hosting a giant bash on this day—bonfires, birthday cake, the whole nine yards! If your church doesn't celebrate, host your own Pentecost extravaganza at home. If you need something a little more low-key, birthday cake (red velvet would be very on theme) or donuts would be just fine. Why donuts? Well, to quote Kendra Tierney, "regular donuts are hole-y and jelly donuts are filled—with the Holy Spirit!"[6] (I know, I even groaned when I typed that. See the recipe on page 200 if you'd like to make your own donuts.)

LITURGY FOR PENTECOST

Before you begin, feel free to light as many candles as you have available. Alternately, enjoy this prayer time around a firepit.

Antiphon

Alleluia! The Spirit of the Lord renews the face of the earth:
O come, let us adore him. Alleluia!

Scripture Readings

John 14:15-17
Acts 2:1-4

Sing Together

"Spirit of the Living God"

Pray

Almighty God, on this day, through the outpouring of the Holy Spirit, you revealed the way of eternal life to every race and nation: Pour out this gift anew, that by the preaching of the Gospel your salvation may reach to the ends of the earth; through Jesus Christ our Lord, who lives and reigns with you, in the unity of the Holy Spirit, one God, for ever and ever. Amen.[7]

ORDINARY TIME

Things take the time they take.
Don't worry.
How many roads did Saint Augustine follow
before he became Saint Augustine?

MARY OLIVER, "DON'T WORRY"

STARTS: Monday after Pentecost

ENDS: Saturday before the first Sunday of Advent

TYPE: Proclamation

DISCIPLINE: Growth

NOTABLE DATES:
Trinity Sunday
Nativity of Saint John the Baptist
Holy Cross Day
Feast of Saint Michael and All Angels
Allhallowtide
Christ the King Sunday

KEY VERSE: "The hour is coming, and is now here, when the true worshipers will worship the Father in spirit and truth, for the Father is seeking such people to worship him" (John 4:23).

HYMN: "Take My Life, and Let It Be"

FRUIT OF THE SPIRIT: Kindness, Goodness, and Gentleness

nd so we come to the season of proclamation that concludes the Cycle of Life. This is a season of practicing resurrection, living out the glorious theology of Eastertide, and embracing God's magnificent plan for our ordinary, everyday life.

History

By the seventh century, most of the church year had been fairly well established. But the question remained—what should the church do between Pentecost and Advent? The obvious answer was *live faithfully*. Go to church and love your neighbor. Go to work and perform your job with integrity. Do justice, love mercy, walk humbly. Get married, make babies, and raise them in the way of the Lord.

While I'd like to tell you this season was named Ordinary Time as a profound theological statement about how God sanctifies all our life and work, alas, that's just not true. It's named Ordinary Time because the weeks after Pentecost are numbered ordinally—first, second, third, and so on. In fact, in many Protestant traditions, it's not actually called Ordinary Time at all but rather the Season after Pentecost or Trinity Season (so named after the First Sunday after Pentecost, Trinity Sunday).

Even so, I like to think the season of Ordinary Time has grown into the theology implied by its name. It's a season that acknowledges and dignifies the growth that comes from everyday faithfulness.

Ordinary Time Places Us in God's Story

For some reason, the word *ordinary* is offensive to some modern sensibilities, conjuring synonymity with mediocre, insipid, or lazy. But it really just means normal, routine, or expected. Most of our lives are incredibly *ordinary*—yard work, meal prep, car maintenance, and so on. Week by week, our lives look much the same—we care for and steward the things God has called us to care for and steward. The ordinariness of a thing, however, does not diminish its sacred place in our lives.

In many ways, Ordinary Time takes us right back to the beginning of God's good story—to Eden. God created the whole world, and then he created humans and said, "Here! Take care of this magnificent garden, tend the fields, eat the fruit, care for the animals, enjoy each other, and walk with me!" God made humans for a very ordinary life—a life of worship lived out through obedience to his commands.

For the Christian, there is no division between secular and sacred—each and every minute is an opportunity for worship. In the foreword of *Every Moment Holy*, Andrew Peterson reminds readers that "there are no unsacred moments; there are only sacred moments and moments we have forgotten are sacred."[1] It's the calling of the Christian to claim (and reclaim) these moments.

The official color of Ordinary Time is green—the color of growth, freshness, and new life. Liturgically, green is the color of the Holy Spirit. Whereas red is the color of the *gifts* of the Holy Spirit, green is the color of the *life* of the Holy Spirit. It's a reminder that the Spirit is the source of all life, and the means by which the life of Christ flows into us.

When Jesus arrived in the tender flesh and blood of an infant, he did so for one reason: to redeem every single part of creation that we might be restored to God, to each other, and to all the created order. God has called us to partner with him in the process of restoring creation fully. In some cases, this means doing the hard work of fixing what has been broken—administering justice, serving the impoverished, alleviating suffering, loving our enemies, restraining evil—but it also means simply having the eyes to see the Lord's kingdom coming through the ordinary means of caring for our neighbors, tending to our family, honoring our parents, and being the church.

> "Whatever you do, in word or deed, do everything in the name of the Lord Jesus, giving thanks to God the Father through him.... Whatever you do, work heartily, as for the Lord and not for men." COLOSSIANS 3:17, 23

It is through the local church that God intends for us to be united with the life of Christ through the sacraments and through fellowship with his body of faithful believers. Scripture is clear that to be in the life of Christ is to be a part of his body (Ephesians 4:4-6; 1 Corinthians 12:12-30; Hebrews 10:24-25). It isn't sexy and it isn't radical. It is, in fact, incredibly ordinary. But the ordinary, local church is the way in which God has called most of us, in our own time and place, to be equipped and strengthened for the work of the kingdom.

And on Sundays, we gather to partake of God's ordinary means of grace—his Word, teaching, fellowship, and of course, the sacraments. Is there anything more ordinary than water, bread, or wine? These are the most basic elements of our common life: water for washing, bread for nourishing, wine for gladdening the heart. But God chooses to reveal himself through these everyday, ordinary components.

In the Anglican tradition, the bread and wine are part of the communal offering each week. Just before collecting a monetary offering, the bread and wine are walked forward to the altar as a symbolic gift to the Lord. The priest then consecrates these elements and offers them back to the congregation—transformed from an offering *to* God into a gift *from* God with an invitation to "feed on him in your hearts by faith, with thanksgiving."

A few years ago, I often baked my church's Communion bread. Each week, I was awed that God allowed me to participate in this glory, taking the humble work of my hands, the basic combination of flour, salt, water, and yeast, blessing it, and then returning it to me as a means of grace. But isn't this just typical of how God works in the world? God takes our modest offerings—our bread and wine, our loaves and fishes, our last coins, meager talents, and willing hearts—and cherishes them, multiplies them, and offers them back to us with more to spare.

Ordinary Time Is a Spiritual Discipline

For each season, I've sought to recommend a spiritual discipline that encourages participants to lean into the themes of that season. Ordinary Time is a little bit different because (1) it's six months long, and (2) a discipline that facilitates growth in one person could be totally different from a discipline that facilitates growth in another. The whole point of Ordinary Time is to seek to grow in the Lord and find, year by year, a more fully abundant life in Christ.

As the "green season," Ordinary Time is for rooting deeper, growing taller, and standing firmer in the life of Christ. This is one reason the cyclical nature of the liturgical year can be so formative: Year by year, we get to retread the track, remembering what God has taught us, living more deeply into the life of Christ, better understanding the work of the Holy Spirit in all seasons. Through these cycles, we become more and more the self that God created us to be—more fully human, more fully integrated into the life of Christ.

As you enter Ordinary Time, prayerfully consider what the Lord has been teaching you about yourself, about your spiritual needs, and about what he is calling you to in this next season. Meditate upon Jesus's words about the Holy Spirit in John 14. In the King James translation, the Holy Spirit is memorably described as our *comforter* (John 14:6). In the seventeenth century, the word "comfort meant to strengthen, energize, convey spiritual power."[2] In this season of the Holy Spirit, pray through what it means to have the Holy Spirit as your comforter—your strength, your energizer, your source of power and life, your catalyst for growth. Express to the Lord your honest desire to grow and listen expectantly for where he calls you.

Ordinary Time Is Communal

If every day were special, no days would be special. After six months packed full of excellent holy days, Ordinary Time is mostly devoid of major feasts, which allows us time and space to enjoy the Lord in the mundane moments of our lives. There are a handful of holidays, but mostly it's a season to be present with God, simply delighting in his will and walking in his ways to the glory of his name.

That being said, there are a few big feasts not to overlook in this season.

Trinity Sunday

Trinity Sunday is celebrated the first Sunday after Pentecost and is unique among church feasts in that it celebrates a *doctrine* rather than an event or saint. This feast is a most excellent pivot for the church year. On the one hand, it invites us to reflect on how the fullness of God has been at work through all time, from the quiet of Advent through the culmination at Pentecost. On the other hand, it reminds us to look for where the fullness of the Trinity is still at work in our own lives.

As far as doctrines go, the Trinity was hard-won. Heresy around this doctrine was rampant in the early church, and while the Trinity is evident throughout the Bible, there's no explicit explanation of it. This doctrine was developed over time by faithful fathers and councils of the church. The Athanasian Creed was penned in the fifth century and is the most complete articulation of the doctrine of the Trinity from the earlier days of the church. It deeply affirms the mystery of the three-in-one, "neither confounding the Persons, nor dividing the Substance."[3]

HELPFUL TRINITY ANALOGIES

The twelfth-century *Scutum Fidei* (Shield of Faith) is a visual way to represent how each of the persons of the Godhead is fully and cohesively God yet also distinct from one another.

In addition to the shield, a significantly earlier and less complex catechetical tool used to affirm the Trinity is that of crossing oneself. The placement of the fingers, often said with the prayer "in the name of the Father, and of the Son, and of the Holy Spirit," is a declaration of the doctrine of the Trinity. While it doesn't *explain* the Trinity, it's a tangible reminder that we are people who love and worship the triune God. Learn more about making the sign of the cross on page 185. This is a great habit to try to develop during Trinity season.

Observing Trinity Sunday

Host a Trini-Tea

The Trinity Season (Ordinary Time) is six months long, so don't feel like you have to do this *on* Trinity Sunday. The theme of a Trini-Tea is, of course, three. Serve three-ingredient sandwiches or three-layer cakes and tarts. Neapolitan ice cream is sure to be a hit, or if you want to be a bit fancier, you could try baking a Neapolitan cake.

Pray

Almighty and everlasting God, you have given to us your servants grace, by the confession of a true faith, to acknowledge the glory of the eternal Trinity, and in the power of your divine Majesty to worship the Unity: Keep us steadfast in this faith and worship, and bring us at last to see you in your one and eternal glory, O Father; who with the Son and the Holy Spirit live and reign, one God, for ever and ever. **Amen.**[4]

Read the Athanasian Creed

It's a long one, and a bit unwieldy to recite in a large group, but it has the fullest explanation of Trinitarian theology of any of the creeds.

Ember Days

While the church calendar doesn't specifically correspond to the seasonal ebbs and flows of creation, there are undoubtedly ways to draw connections between the turning seasons of the earth and the themes of the liturgical year in the Northern Hemisphere.[5] For instance, there are definite parallels between the silence of Advent and the darkness of winter. In the same way, Lent is a season for tilling the soil of our hearts and planting seeds of faith much like spring is for literal sowing. Ordinary Time is a growing season, like summer, and God willing, it is a harvest season, like fall.

The church has traditionally marked this changing of the seasons by remembering four sets of Ember Days (or Embertides). These are days set aside in each earthly season to fast and pray for the leadership of the church. While Ember Days are primarily used in liturgical traditions as days to intercede specifically for those receiving Holy Orders (such as ordination to the priesthood, deaconate, or bishopric), there is always wisdom in praying for the faithful stewardship of your congregation. It is easy to understand the work of church leaders in agrarian terms—they weed, sow, water, wait, and harvest. They are spiritual gardeners, called to tend to and cultivate God's people through seasons of planting, growing, harvesting, and resting. How appropriate that we especially pray for them at the turn of each earthly season.

Ember Days are observed...

- In summer, on the Wednesday, Friday, and Saturday after the Day of Pentecost
- In fall, on the Wednesday, Friday, and Saturday following Holy Cross Day (September 14)
- In winter, on the Wednesday, Friday, and Saturday following Saint Lucy's Day (December 13)
- In spring, on the Wednesday, Friday, and Saturday following the first Sunday in Lent

Observing Ember Days

Consider fasting on these days that your hunger may serve as a reminder to pray for the leaders of the church. These days are also a great opportunity to write a note of thanks to your leaders or perhaps to bake some cookies for them.

Prayer for Ember Days

Almighty God, the giver of all good gifts, in your divine providence you have appointed various orders in your Church: Give your grace, we humbly pray, to all who are called to any office and ministry for your people; and so fill them with the truth of your doctrine and clothe them with holiness of life, that they may faithfully serve before you, to the glory of your great Name and for the benefit of your holy Church; through Jesus Christ our Lord, who lives and reigns with you, in the unity of the Holy Spirit, one God, now and for ever. **Amen.**[6]

Nativity of Saint John the Baptist—June 24

John the Baptist—the prophet to come like Elijah (Malachi 4:5) and the first prophet in Israel in over 400 years—was the cousin and forerunner of Jesus. Since the earliest days of the church, John the Baptist has been honored. Francis Weiser reports that "fifteen churches were dedicated to him in the ancient imperial city of Constantinople."[7] At the Council of Agde in AD 506, it was determined that this feast was one of the highest of the year and would have three masses just like Christmas.

Celebrating John the Baptist

Burn

Because John's feast day is so close to the summer solstice (June 21), the day was celebrated throughout Europe with large bonfires on hilltops and mountains. Often these fires were accompanied by large festivals. It's a great night to host a cookout and enjoy a bonfire or backyard firepit. Don't forget to bless your fire!

BLESSING THE FIRE

Our help is in the name of the Lord
Who made heaven and earth.

Almighty God, source of all light, bless and sanctify these flames that they may be to us a source of light and warmth. Refine us by the fire of your love that we may shine forth your light in the world as a beacon on a hill. Grant us grace to one day come into the presence of your perpetual light; through Jesus Christ our Lord. Amen.

Pray

Almighty God, by whose providence your servant John the Baptist was wonderfully born, and sent to prepare the way of your Son our Savior by preaching repentance: Make us so to follow his teaching and holy life, that we may truly repent, boldly rebuke vice, patiently suffer for the sake of truth, and proclaim the coming of Jesus Christ our Lord; who lives and reigns with you and the Holy Spirit, one God, for ever and ever. **Amen.**[8]

Holy Cross Day

Most traditions celebrate Holy Cross Day on September 14. While Good Friday is for celebrating Christ's finished work on the cross, Holy Cross Day (also known as the Exaltation or Triumph of the Holy Cross) celebrates the icon of the cross itself. In the first century, the cross represented Roman brutality, oppression, and death. By dying on the cross and rising again, Jesus turned that meaning on its head, transforming the cross into the path to life and freedom. In the centuries following the crucifixion, the cross became a sign of God's work in the world and the glorious way he turns everything upside down—the first shall be last, the lowly shall be exalted, the foolish shall shame the wise, God's power is perfected in weakness, and in death there is new and everlasting life. The cross is an image of how God can redeem even the very worst of humanity and of how strength and victory come in weakness.

Some variation of the cross was deeply associated with Christianity by the early second century—these variations were usually related to Greek letters used as abbreviations for *Christ, Jesus,* or *cross.* A symbol called a staurogram was used in texts to represent the crucifixion. It was made by combining the Greek letters for *tau* and *rho,* creating an abbreviation of *stauros*—the Greek word for "cross."

Another way in which crosses were used by early Christians was in the practice of crossing oneself. In AD 204, Tertullian describes what was already a common ritual among Christians: tracing the cross on their foreheads multiple times per day.[9] From its earliest days, crossing oneself was a physical prayer, a reminder of being set apart, walking in and under Christ's cross. Making the sign over a person or an object was a physical way of sanctifying that thing, of marking it as Christ's—an instrument for his glory. More than 1,300 years later, in his smaller catechism, Martin Luther recommends making a habit of crossing oneself upon waking and just before going to sleep as a reminder to go forth into the day in the power of Christ and in the evening to enter into his rest.

While there are some who may see this action as superstitious, for most people it's a genuine prayer of their heart, an outward expression of their inward desire for Christ to be over and through them. It's similar to the physical communication of a kiss or the physical worship of kneeling or raising hands—though silent, it is no less meaningful a gesture than those made of words.

HOW AND WHEN TO CROSS YOURSELF

There are numerous appropriate ways to cross yourself. But for teaching and reminding purposes, I'm only going to give you one: When you cross yourself, you place your thumb, index, and middle finger together to represent the Trinity. Your ring and pinky finger touch your palm to represent the two natures of Christ—fully God and fully man.

To cross yourself, start at your forehead, move down to your sternum, then across to your left shoulder, across to your right shoulder, and back to the center. Though forehead crossing was common in the early church, a larger gesture became necessary as congregations grew larger and priests were therefore farther away from their congregants.

While you can cross yourself any time you feel the need to make such a gesture of prayer, it's most common to cross yourself at the invocation of the Father (forehead), Son (sternum), and Holy Spirit (left and right shoulders). Supposedly this is a symbol of the Father in heaven when you touch your forehead, the Son coming to earth as the downward movement indicates incarnation, and the power of the Holy Spirit within as you cross your own shoulders. It's likely, however, that someone invented this symbolism to match the larger gesture rather than invented the gesture to convey the symbolism.

It's also totally appropriate to cross someone or something you're praying over: your children, your home, your workspace, or anything else you'd like to physically commit to Christ's care.

Observing Holy Cross Day

Cross Yourself

If you don't already do so, perhaps make a practice of crossing yourself. Like a lot of habits, it can be a bit awkward at first if you're not accustomed to it. In time, however, you'll likely find this gesture to be deeply meaningful in your prayer life.

Pray

Almighty God, whose Son our Savior Jesus Christ was lifted high upon the cross that he might draw the whole world to himself: Mercifully grant that we, who glory in the mystery of our redemption, may have grace to take up our cross and follow him; who lives and reigns with you and the Holy Spirit, one God, in glory everlasting. **Amen.**[10]

Sing Together

"When I Survey the Wonderous Cross" or "Lift High the Cross"

Saint Michael and All Angels—September 29

The Feast of Saint Michael and All Angels—also known as Michaelmas—has been celebrated by the church since the fourth century. This ancient feast is pulled from Revelation 12:7-9, in which Michael defeats Satan and throws him to earth. For his skill in battle, Saint Michael is considered a great defender of the church and the greatest of the archangels.

Celebrating Michaelmas

Eat

As the story goes, when Satan landed on earth, he landed in a thorny blackberry patch. Satan cursed the fruit, stamping and spitting on it. As such, September 29 is the last day of the year for Christians to "safely" enjoy blackberries. It's customary on this day to enjoy blackberry pastries (see the recipe on page 188) and desserts, make blackberry jam, and cook a goose glazed with blackberry. Alternately, make a devil's food cake and "slay" it with the serving knife (then let your children enjoy it with cocktail swords). Angel food cake and deviled eggs would also be on theme.

Pray

Everlasting God, you have ordained and constituted in a wonderful order the ministries of angels and mortals: Mercifully grant that, as your holy angels always serve and worship you in heaven, so by your appointment they may help and defend us here on earth: through Jesus Christ our Lord, who lives and reigns with you and the Holy Spirit, one God, for ever and ever. **Amen.**[11]

Allhallowtide—October 31 to November 2

Allhallowtide is discussed in detail starting on page 193.

Christ the King Sunday

Celebrated the last Sunday before Advent, Christ the King Sunday is the final Sunday of the liturgical year. This is, by far, the newest addition to the church year, having been added to the calendar in 1925 (no, that's not a typo!) by Pope Pius XI. He may have instituted this feast to "combat what he considered the destructive forces of this age...[and] to reassure the faithful that Christ the King was still in control."[12]

While Ascension Day is very much the true celebration of Christ the King, Christ's reign is an appropriate theme to both begin and end Ordinary Time. It also leads nicely into Advent's theme of preparing our hearts for Christ's return. Since this Sunday is so near Thanksgiving, it can be a challenge to do anything particularly special to celebrate the day. If you have the bandwidth to make a king cake, chicken à la king, or some other royal-themed food, go for it. If you don't, simply go to church and bask in the glory of serving and worshipping the King of kings.

Prayer for Christ the King Sunday

Almighty and everlasting God, whose will it is to restore all things in your well-beloved Son, the King of kings, and Lord of lords: Mercifully grant that the peoples of the earth, divided and enslaved by sin, may be freed and brought together under his most gracious rule; who lives and reigns with you and the Holy Spirit, one God, now and for ever. **Amen.**[13]

Sing Together

"Holy God, We Praise Thy Name."
This hymn is based on an ancient prayer called the Te Deum Laudamus, *meaning "We Praise You, O God." It is traditionally sung or said on Christ the King Sunday.*

BLACKBERRY PIE

Servings: 10

INGREDIENTS

Crust:

2¼ cups all-purpose flour, plus some for dusting work surface

2 tsp. sugar

1 tsp. salt

1 cup (16 T.) cold butter, cut into pieces

6 to 8 T. ice water

1 egg

2 T. turbinado (or granulated) sugar

Filling:

5 to 6 cups fresh or frozen blackberries (if using frozen berries, do *not* thaw them)

¾ cup sugar

¼ cup instant tapioca

2 T. lemon juice

½ tsp. ground nutmeg

¼ tsp. allspice

DIRECTIONS

1. First prepare the crust. In a large bowl, combine the flour, sugar, and salt. Cut the butter into small pieces and use a pastry blender or food processor to cut it into the flour, until you have pea-size pieces. Next, use your hands to mix in water, a tablespoon at a time, until your pie crust comes together and is not dry. Take care not to overwork the dough, in order to retain a light, flaky crust.

2. Divide the dough in half, shape it into two balls, and wrap each crust ball tightly in plastic wrap. Chill it in the freezer for 10 minutes or in the refrigerator for 30 minutes before use.

3. Meanwhile, preheat the oven to 400°F, and prepare the pie filling. In a large bowl, combine all the filling ingredients, using a little more or less sugar based on your preference and the sweetness or tartness of your blackberries.

4. Roll out the bottom pie crust on a lightly floured surface. Place it into a pie plate. Gently pour the berry mixture into the pie shell.

5. Add more flour to your rolling surface if needed, then roll out the top crust. Slice the top crust into long strips about 1 inch wide with a pizza cutter. Place 5 to 6 strips one way across the pie, then weave the 5 or 6 remaining crust strips the opposite direction until you've covered the pie with a nice lattice.

6. Put the egg into a small dish and whisk the yolk and white together. Brush the top crust with the egg and sprinkle it with turbinado sugar.

7. Place the pie pan on a baking sheet lined with parchment paper.

8. The total bake time will be about 70 minutes. Start checking it around 30 minutes, and once it is nicely browned, cover the pie loosely with aluminum foil, being sure there is an air vent for steam to escape. This will keep the crust from burning while it finishes baking. Bake until the pie filling is bubbling.

9. Remove the pie from the oven and let it cool before you slice it. Serve with vanilla ice cream!

Adapted with gratitude from Jessica Robinson, A Farmgirl's Kitchen

LITURGY FOR ORDINARY TIME

Since Ordinary Time is so long, I am not recommending any particular Scripture passages for the weeks of this season. Read through a book of the Bible as a family or read a storybook Bible. Before your weekly reading, light a candle. The words in **bold** are intended for everyone to say together as they are able.

Opening

"The hour is coming, and is now here, when the true worshipers will worship the Father in spirit and truth, for the Father is seeking such people to worship him" (John 4:23).

Antiphon

Create in me a clean heart, O God,
   and renew a right spirit within me.
Cast me not away from your presence,
   and take not your Holy Spirit from me.
Restore to me the joy of your salvation,
   and uphold me with a willing spirit.

Scripture Reading

Choose your own or read Ephesians 2:4-10.

Sing Together

"Take My Life, and Let It Be" or another favorite hymn of your choice

Pray

If you'd like, take this time to pray as a family, lifting up your own needs and the needs of your community.

Lord's Prayer

Closing Prayer for Morning

O Lord, our heavenly Father, almighty and everlasting God, you have brought us safely to the beginning of this day: Defend us by your mighty power that we may not fall into sin nor run into any danger; and that, guided by your Spirit, we may do what is righteous in your sight; through Jesus Christ our Lord. **Amen.**[14]

Closing Prayer for Evening

Lord Jesus, stay with us, for evening is at hand and the day is past; be our companion in the way, kindle our hearts, and awaken hope, that we may know you as you are revealed in Scripture and the breaking of bread. Grant this for the sake of your love. **Amen.**[15]

ALLHALLOWTIDE

Teach me to live, that I may dread
the grave as little as my bed.
Teach me to die, that so I may
rise glorious at the judgment day.

Thomas Ken, "All Praise to Thee,
My God, This Night"

STARTS: October 31

ENDS: November 2

TYPE: Proclamation

DISCIPLINE: memento mori and Examen

NOTABLE DATES:
All Saints' Day

KEY VERSE: "Teach us to number our days that we may get a heart of wisdom" (Psalm 90:12).

HYMN: "For All the Saints"

Allhallowtide is best known by its component parts: Halloween, All Saints' Day, and All Souls' Day. Of all the 'tides of the liturgical year, this one is probably the most controversial and divisive among Christians, with some camps opting to ignore its existence altogether and others leaning in 110 percent.

History

First, a bit of history: The origin of All Saints' Day in the West can be traced to the many separate celebrations of local martyrs of the early church. Even before the legalization of Christianity in the Roman Empire in the fourth century, Christians would often gather at the gravesites of their community's martyrs to remember and celebrate their lives, taking courage from their witness to live boldly for Christ. As the church grew and the theology and traditions of Christianity became increasingly codified for the sake of consistent practice and orthodox belief across space and time, the commemoration of every single martyr by the whole church became impossible.

In the early seventh century, Pope Boniface IV converted the Pantheon in Rome to a church, dedicating it on May 13 to Saint Mary and all martyrs.

This day was to be celebrated annually as the feast of *all* martyrs, effectively consolidating various local martyr celebrations into one holy day acknowledged by the whole church. Eventually, this day expanded to become the Feast of All Hallows (*Hallows* meaning "Saints"), a celebration that encompassed the twelve apostles, saints, martyrs, and confessors (those who stood firm in their faith despite serious opposition but were not martyred). The Feast of All Hallows was moved to November 1 by Pope Gregory IV in AD 835. Like all great Christian feasts, its celebration began the evening before. Thus, October 31 became known as the vigil of All Hallows' Eve, which was eventually shortened to "Halloween."

ISN'T HALLOWEEN A REPACKAGED PAGAN FESTIVAL?

In the twentieth century, the claim that Halloween is thoroughly pagan, originating at the ancient Celtic festival of Samhain (pronounced "sah'-wən"), has become widely spread and frequently parroted. This is simply not true.

Reliable scholarship in anthropology, archeology, literature, and history will tell you that all we really know about ancient Samhain festivals is that around late October or early November there was often a large feast and bonfire to mark the end of the harvest season and the start of winter. Considering that similar harvest festivals were popular across Europe, there's no reason to believe that Samhain was singled out as a "pagan" feast that needed "Christianization."

Halloween definitely has its origin with the church!

Unfortunately, the understanding of *saint* by the medieval church was much narrower than the actual New Testament use of *saint* and encompassed only a couple hundred people of extraordinary witness. As such, about 300 years after the institution of All Saints' Day on November 1, the celebration of All Souls' Day was tacked on to the festivities on November 2 as a commemoration of *all* the faithful departed—the whole "cloud of witnesses" (Hebrews 12:1), as the case may be.

Most regrettably, the limited understanding of *saint* wasn't the only misguided piece of theology woven into Allhallowtide. Both All Hallows' Eve and All Souls' Day originally focused heavily on the doctrine of Purgatory (the idea that before a faithful departed soul can enter paradise, it must undergo further refinement, slowly working off sin before being admitted to God's presence).

When the Protestant Reformation arrived in the sixteenth century, the customs and meaning around Allhallowtide changed significantly, with some reformers shifting the focus toward a more traditional understanding of the afterlife as recorded in the Apostles' Creed: I believe in "the communions of saints, the forgiveness of sins, the resurrection of the body, and the life everlasting." In addition to doing away with the doctrine of purgatory, the Reformation shifted three things for the Christian understanding of *saints*:

- Reassigned all faithful believers the proper title of saint
- Reaffirmed that the "communion of saints" is comprised of both the living community around us and those who have died and gone to glory ahead of us
- Reinstated *all* the faithful departed as the "great cloud of witnesses" who surround us, support us, and encourage us (Hebrews 12:1-2)

These theological shifts have comfortably allowed for the endurance of the Feasts of All Saints and All Souls (with some changes to what each day emphasizes) but left Halloween as an open question.

REFORMATION DAY

On October 31, 1517, Martin Luther tacked his Ninety-Five Theses to the door of a church in Wittenberg. As it turned out, this simple, common bit of community life became a movement that would reshape the church. Though some traditions celebrate Reformation Day on October 31, this practice deserves deeper consideration. Undoubtedly, there are many good, healthy reforms that came out of this movement, but a grievous schism within the body of Christ also occurred. In our remembrance of the Reformation, it's important to hold the hard and painful in tension with the beneficial and necessary.

Here's the good news: The church has another way to celebrate this day. Nearly 1,000 years before the Reformation, the church began celebrating Allhallowtide as three days set aside for remembering and celebrating the witness of all faithful people. It is a most fitting time to remember the work of Martin Luther and other Reformation theologians alongside saints of every age.

Allhallowtide Places Us in God's Story

These three days sit squarely in the confines of Ordinary Time, a funny little 'tide unto itself in the midst of six months of growth and life. Much of the church year focuses on the big picture of God's work in the world. But on the cusp of both winter and Advent, the church invites its people to a very personal autumn triduum with three days to reflect upon the end of our own lives, the end of our days in service to the gospel and church militant, and our future in the church triumphant.

As the darkness lingers in the morning and comes quickly in the evening, the cold sweeps in, the earth hardens, and creation preaches...death. Fall is earth's reminder of our mortality and of the death-to-life journey to which God mercifully calls each of us. This sermon is far less welcome in our hearts than spring's good news. We try to put a costume on this lesson with sweaters and boots, pumpkin spice everything, steaming bowls of soup, and blazing fireplaces—but the deadness is inescapable. Allhallowtide arrives to tap us on the shoulder, inviting us into this seasonal death with open arms, exclaiming, "*Memento mori!* Remember you will die."

Perhaps this seems morbid to you. After all, we live in a world that actively seeks to ignore the reality of death. But memento mori is a reminder of this relatively obvious fact: Life is short, we will all die. So *how do we prepare for a holy death?*

It's a question that starts in the Garden of Eden, is echoed through the Old Testament, proclaimed again by Christ, and asked anew in our own lives. Psalms 90:12 perhaps summarizes memento mori best: "Teach us to number our days that we may get a heart of wisdom." The autumn triduum is an invitation to a three-day reflection to help us number our days that we may be wise.

On Halloween, we remember that we must literally die. Are we ready?

On All Saints' Day, we remember that, God willing, we will rise again to newness of life. Are we fixing our eyes on Christ that we might run with endurance, storing up treasure in heaven along the way?

On All Souls' Day, we remember that no one escapes death. Are we making the most of what God has given us?

Allhallowtide Is a Spiritual Discipline

Jesus spent his whole life preparing for his death and much of his ministry preparing his disciples for his death. He was the child born to die. His teaching, his example, his love would have all been a footnote in history apart from his death and resurrection. If a spiritual discipline is doing the things Jesus did, then memento mori, remembering and preparing for your death, is a spiritual discipline.

One way to consciously practice memento mori is through the exercise of the examen. The examen is a spiritual practice that originated with Saint Ignatius Loyola (1491–1556). It requires the participants to "listen deeply to the data of our lives"[1]—attending to mental, emotional, spiritual, and physical states. The practice of examen asks you to reflect on a set of "high/low" questions, for example:

- Where did I feel the most loved today? Where did I feel least loved?

- When did I feel most deeply connected to God today? When did I feel most disconnected?

- When did I best love God and my neighbor today? When did I least love God and my neighbor today?

- Which parts of my day helped me prepare for eternity? Which parts did not?

The set of questions can be adapted to suit the timing and the needs of your soul. They are also a wonderful reflective conversational tool to use with your family. Simplifying the questions to "What made you happy today?" and "What made you sad today?" can be a lovely way to attend to the spirits of your children, and to know how to pray with and for them.

At Allhallowtide, an examen specifically focused on memento mori is a helpful way to attend to your eternal needs. For some, the practice of memento mori is a daily, weekly, or seasonal exercise (it's quite appropriate for Lent as well), but if that's overwhelming, perhaps an annual reflection will serve. The goal of both memento mori and the examen is to bring you to a greater awareness of the Lord's work in yourself.

Allhallowtide Is Communal
Halloween

Over the past one hundred years, Halloween has undeniably morphed into an almost totally secular holiday focused on community traditions rather than on its historic function in the church. (Halloween, unlike Christmas, had no significant tie to the life of Christ to help it withstand its near-total secularization.) Vestiges of its origin, however, are still visible in the traditions of costumes and trick-or-treating. Originally, the poor of the community would go "souling" on All Hallows' Eve, traveling door-to-door promising to pray for the souls of a home's deceased family members in exchange for a soul cake (a shortbread-type cookie with dried fruit and nuts). Both the beggars and the wealthy at home would dress in disguise so that they could give "in accordance with the anonymity recommended in the Gospel. Begging, disguise, and generosity hence performed a multiple function in binding together the sundered realms of the rich and poor, the living and the dead...in a single community of grace."[2]

While ultimately the observance of Halloween is a matter of Christian conscience, for the modern church and the Christian family, Halloween need not be a pagan holiday built around fear and the paranormal, but rather considered as a secular holiday (like Fourth of July or Memorial Day) focused on generosity and joy. Both Christian churches and Christian homes can open their doors on Halloween in a posture of welcome, delighting in the opportunity to love neighbors well while both accepting and providing hospitality. While your children may not be down-on-their-luck street rats in need of the sustenance of a soul cake, allowing them to trick-or-treat in costumes for candy is its own participation in the community of grace, a common ground drawing neighbor to neighbor and home to home in an increasingly divided world.

MEMENTO MORI DONUTS

At some point, souling on Halloween started getting a little out of hand, becoming a rowdy and irreverent affair for people who wanted free food. One woman, fed up with this nonsense, started cutting holes in the middle of her soul cakes and frying them. She would hand these deep-fried rings to her "soulers," asking them to meditate on their eternal souls as they enjoyed their donuts. The treat's ring shape was a symbol of eternity and the fact that they were hot...well, I'll let you draw your own conclusion. Regardless, a more delicious memento mori reflection has yet to be invented!

If your family can't (or shouldn't) eat a dozen donuts in one sitting, you can freeze the cut-out donuts after the second rise. Just thaw them completely and fry them when you're ready to eat! These are tastiest on the day they're fried.

Servings: about 1 dozen

INGREDIENTS

Donuts:
1¼ cups milk
2¼ tsp. (1 packet) active dry yeast
2 eggs
8 T. (1 stick) melted butter
¼ cup granulated sugar
1 tsp. salt
4 cups all-purpose flour, plus more for rolling
    out the dough
2 quarts neutral oil for frying

Glaze:
¼ cup whole milk
1 tsp. vanilla extract
2 cups powdered sugar

DIRECTIONS

1. In a small saucepan, heat the milk until it is warm but not hot (you should see small bubbles forming near the edge of the saucepan, and it should not be too hot when a drop is placed on the inside of your wrist). In a large bowl, combine the warmed milk with the yeast, stir it lightly and let it sit until the mixture is foamy, about 5 minutes.

2. Using a mixer fitted with a dough hook, beat the eggs, butter, sugar, and salt into the yeast mixture. Add two cups of flour and mix until combined, then mix in 2 more cups of flour until the dough pulls away from the sides of the bowl. Add more flour,

a tablespoon at a time, if the dough is too wet. If you're using an electric mixer, the dough will probably become too thick to beat; when it does, transfer it to a floured surface and gently knead it until smooth. Remove the dough from the bowl, grease the bowl with a little oil, then return the dough to the bowl and cover. Let the dough rise at room temperature until it doubles in size, about 1 hour.

3. Turn the dough out onto a well-floured surface and roll it to a ½-inch thickness. Cut out the donuts with a donut cutter, flouring the cutter between each donut. You can also use a clean, empty tin can (about 3-inch diameter) and a narrow bottle cap (about 1-inch diameter) to cut out the donuts and holes. Reserve the donut holes, but knead the scraps together, let the dough sit a few moments, and then reroll the dough to cut more donuts.

4. Put the donuts and holes on floured baking sheets, allowing room for expansion. Cover the donuts and let them rise in a warm place until they are slightly puffed up, about 45 minutes.

5. After about half an hour, put the oil in a heavy-bottomed pot or Dutch oven over medium heat until it reaches 375°. Prepare trays or cooling racks to receive the cooked donuts by lining them with paper towels.

6. Test the oil temperature with a donut hole, cooking it for about 45 seconds per side, let it cool on your rack briefly, and check the inside. If it browns too fast, the oil is too hot. If it browns too slowly, the oil is not hot enough. Adjust the temperature slightly, wait a few minutes, then try again. (You can also use a wooden spoon handle to check temperature if you do not have a thermometer. Dip the handle into the oil. If the oil bubbles steadily, then it's ready to fry. If the oil bubbles very quickly, it is too hot.)

7. When your oil is ready, use your fingers or a slotted metal spatula to carefully pick up and add the donuts to the oil a few at a time. Don't crowd the pan! Fry for 45 to 60 seconds, until the bottoms are deep golden, then use a slotted spoon to flip them and continue cooking until they're a uniform color. Donut holes cook faster. Transfer the donuts to the prepared plates or racks and repeat the process with the rest of the dough, adjusting the heat as needed to keep the oil at 375°.

8. If you want powdered sugar or cinnamon sugar donuts, toss the donuts in the desired coating while they are still warm and serve them as soon as possible. If you are glazing the donuts, allow them to cool a little before glazing.

9. Whisk together all the glaze ingredients in a bowl that is just wide enough to dip the top of the donuts into the glaze. Alternately, you can drizzle the glaze over the top of the donuts. Add sprinkles for extra fun! Then wait about five minutes for the glaze to set and enjoy!

Adapted with gratitude from New York Times Cooking

Jack-O'-Lanterns

Irish legend has it that there was once a trickster named Jack who came across Satan in a tree. He whipped out his knife and carved crosses into the tree's trunk, effectively trapping Satan in its branches. In exchange for never having to go to hell, Jack released the devil. When Jack finally died, he was sent to hell for his wickedness, but Satan wouldn't admit him. He chucked Jack's soul back to earth and tossed a coal of hellfire after him for good measure. Jack put the coal in a turnip and used this lantern to light his eternal wanderings across the earth.

Eventually Irish migrants to America realized that carving pumpkins was *way* easier than carving turnips, and jack-o'-lanterns became an annual pumpkin-carving event. For a *wonderful* Christian take on the tradition, I would recommend reading *The Pumpkin Patch Parable* by Liz Curtis Higgins. My family reads this together each year before we carve our pumpkins, and we remember how God gives us his own light to shine to the world.

LITURGY FOR CARVING PUMPKINS

Assemble your pumpkin-carving materials plus candles and a lighter. The words in **bold** are intended for everyone to say together as they are able.

Blessed are you, O King of the universe, who brings forth pumpkins from the earth to sustain our bodies and gladden our hearts; through Jesus Christ our Lord. Amen.

Carve your pumpkins and place an unlit candle inside each one.

Create in me a clean heart, O God,

And renew a right spirit within me.

Light the pumpkins' candles:

O Lord, we thank you that you have seen us and known us, sought us and bought us, and cleaned us of all unrighteousness. Grant us grace to be bearers of your light that we may illuminate the dark places and draw others to your glory; through Jesus Christ our Lord. Amen.

All Saints' Day and All Souls' Day

Functionally, All Saints' Day and All Souls' Day (also known as the Commemoration of the Faithful Departed) are very similar—on both days we remember and celebrate the great cloud of witnesses.

On All Saints' Day, the church community broadly remembers all who have been faithful witnesses for the church, and especially celebrates those who have had outstanding influence in its theology and traditions. On this day, it is customary to pray the Litany of the Saints. While the litany may seem long, it's humbling and inspiring to read this short (historically speaking!) list of the faithful. What an honor to be numbered among them. We give glory to God for those he raises up in every generation to lead by example.

On All Souls' Day we turn our attention to those who have had an extraordinary witness in our own lives, giving glory to God for the family members, friends, and teachers who have supported us by their own faith and courage.

All Saints' Day is one of the most significant feasts of the church year—and All Souls' Day is close on its heels—because "it celebrates what could have been impossible. The cross is the tree that bears fruit. This is the feast of its harvest."[3] On these days, we celebrate all God's wondrous work in the world through the body of Christ—his church. As we praise God for those who have run the race ahead of us, we ask that God may grant us the grace to follow in their footsteps and act as faithful witnesses in our own time.

Feast like a Saint

All Saints' Day is a glorious feast to celebrate at home. As those who have gone before sit at the overflowing table of our Father's bounty, so we look forward to one day sitting there with them at our own feast. If you can swing it, make a "fancy" meal for your family on November 1 (or the nearest weekend). You may define *fancy* however you'd like—just do something special and point those you feast with to the beautiful heavenly banquet that is to come.

Dress like a Saint

If you're looking for fun Halloween costumes, dressing like your favorite saint is a great way to go. This is also a wonderful opportunity to learn more about the saints. Everyone in the family can dress as their favorite saint and tell the family a little about him or her. You could even make it a game where someone gives clues about who they are dressed as and everyone else has to guess. This idea also adapts well to a party.

Remember Recently Deceased Saints

All Souls' Day is an opportunity to honor people who have made a lasting impact on your faith and remember those saints who have passed into glory since the last Allhallowtide. It's not uncommon to visit graves on this day, bringing flowers or favorite foods to "share" in honor of these loved ones. If such a visit is not possible, you can instead eat their favorite foods. Pull out their photos, light a candle for each person you're honoring, and share stories of what you loved about them. In your prayers, thank God for their light and life and for the hope of eternity with them.

PRAYER FOR ALL SOULS' DAY

Almighty God, you have surrounded us with a great cloud of witnesses: Grant that we, encouraged by the good example of your servant [name], may persevere in running the race that is set before us, until at last, with him/her, we attain to your eternal joy; through Jesus Christ, the pioneer and perfecter of our faith, who lives and reigns with you and the Holy Spirit, one God, for ever and ever. **Amen.**[4]

LITURGY FOR ALLHALLOWTIDE

There are readings for each day of Allhallowtide. Before you begin, light a candle and open your Bible to the day's reading. The words in **bold** are intended for everyone to say together as they are able.

Opening
"The hour is coming, and is now here, when the true worshipers will worship the Father in spirit and truth, for the Father is seeking such people to worship him" (John 4:23).

Antiphon
The Lord is glorious in his saints:
O come, let us adore him.

Te Deum Laudamus ("We Praise You, O God")
We praise you, O God; we acclaim you as Lord;
   All creation worships you, the Father everlasting.
To you all angels, all the powers of heaven,
   the cherubim and seraphim, sing in endless praise:
Holy, Holy, Holy, Lord God of power and might,
   heaven and earth are full of your glory.
The glorious company of apostles praise you.
   The noble fellowship of prophets praise you.
The white-robed army of martyrs praise you.
   Throughout the world the holy church acclaims you:
   Father, of majesty unbounded,
Your true and only Son, worthy of all praise,
   And the Holy Spirit, advocate and guide.
You, Christ, are the King of glory,
   the eternal Son of the Father.

When you took our flesh to set us free
    you humbly chose the Virgin's womb.
You overcame the sting of death
    and opened the kingdom of heaven to all believers.
You are seated at God's right hand in glory.
    We believe that you will come to be our judge.
Come then, Lord, and help your people,
    Bought with the price of your own blood,
and bring us with your saints
    To glory everlasting.

Scripture Reading

Anyone may do the reading. Once the reading has finished, perhaps take a minute to discuss and reflect on it together.

1. Halloween—Matthew 5:1-13
2. All Saints' Day—Revelation 7:9-17
3. All Souls' Day—Ephesians 1:15-23

Sing Together

"For All the Saints"

Pray

In addition, take this time to pray as a family, lifting up your own needs and the needs of your community.

Lord's Prayer

On All Saints' Day, add the Litany of Saints here.

Closing Prayer

Almighty God, you have knit together your elect in one communion and fellowship in the mystical Body of your Son: Give us grace so to follow your blessed saints in all virtuous and godly living, that we may come to those ineffable joys that you have prepared for those who truly love you; through Jesus Christ our Lord, who with you and the Holy Spirit lives and reigns, one God, in glory everlasting. Amen.[5]

Litany of Saints

The Litany of Saints is traditionally prayed on All Saints' Day, though you should feel free to use it any time it is helpful. This prayer gives glory to God for the faithfulness of over sixty specific saints from the first centuries of the church. For Protestant use, I recommend the Reformed Litany of Saints by Reverend Ben Jeffries, which is available online.[6]

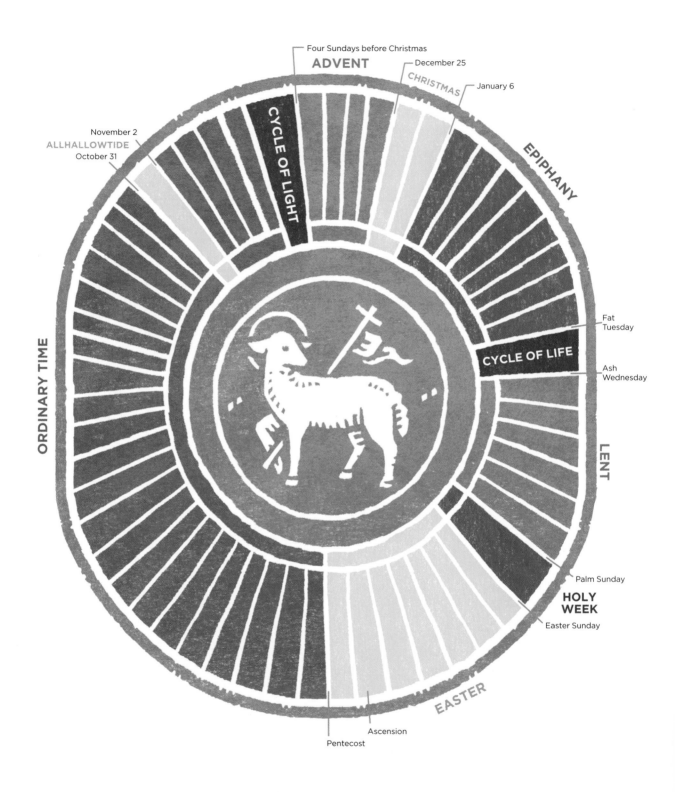

BENEDICTION

*I pray that you, being rooted and established in love, may have power, together
with all the Lord's holy people, to grasp how wide and long and high and
deep is the love of Christ, and to know this love that surpasses knowledge—
that you may be filled to the measure of all the fullness of God.*

Ephesians 3:17-19 NIV

The church year is visualized as a circle—a reminder that the discipline of remembrance is a *Cycle* of Grace. While the seasons repeat every year, the experiences of each annual cycle layer on one another, drawing deeper connections to Scripture in our hearts and minds, drawing us closer to God in Spirit and in truth as we remember—make present—the life of Christ and the coming Kingdom in our hearts and our homes year after year.

As you enter into a new cycle, may you discover that by God's grace, you have grown and changed for the better, and are growing and changing still.

May you practice the same liturgies, repeat the same traditions, pray the same prayers, and read the same scriptures and be surprised to learn something new.

And may you be increasingly shaped, year by year, into the likeness of Christ.

Amen.

NOTES

Keep Sacred Time

1   Gemma Curtis, "Your Life in Numbers," Dreams, April 28, 2021, https://www.dreams.co.uk/sleep-matters-club/your-life-in-numbers-infographic.

2. Annie Dillard, *The Writing Life* (New York: HarperCollins, 1989), 32.

3. Eugene H. Peterson, *Working the Angles* (Grand Rapids, MI: Eerdmans, 1987), 68.

4. Johan Kahl (1721–1746), "Arise, My Soul, Arise."

5. "But what about the practice of taking a Sabbath rest once a week?" you may ask. It's a great question and one that I cannot fully treat in this chapter or this book. You can, however, read some additional thoughts on Sabbath on pages 150-151.

6. Because the eighth day of the week is considered the eighth day of (new) creation, baptismal fonts—holding the water of rebirth—are often octagonal, a nod to the new creation one becomes upon being baptized. See Romans 6:3-5.

7. Laurence Hull Stookey, *Calendar: Christ's Time for the Church* (Nashville, TN: Abingdon Press, 1996), 41.

Train for Righteousness

1. James K.A. Smith, *You Are What You Love* (Grand Rapids, MI: Brazos Press, 2016), 13, 15. "You are what you love because you live toward what you *want*." "To be human is to be a lover and to love something ultimate."

2. Patricia B. Buckland, *Advent to Pentecost: A History of the Christian Year* (Wilton, CT: Morehouse-Barlow, 1979), 23.

Live the Liturgy

1. Smith, *What You Love*, 79.

2. Smith, *What You Love*, 79.

3. Jaroslav Pelikan, *The Vindication of Tradition: The 1983 Jefferson Lecture in the Humanities* (New Haven, CT: Yale University Press, 1984), 65.

4. Philip H. Pfatteicher, *Journey into the Heart of God: Living the Liturgical Year* (New York: Oxford University Press, 2013), 326, 328.

Advent

1. The lectionary is a set of preselected and scheduled Scripture readings for use in both personal and communal worship. It generally runs in a three-year cycle, and readings are selected based on their suitability to themes of the liturgical seasons.

2. Angelus Silesius, *The Cherubinic Wanderer*, trans. Maria Shrady (Mahwah, NJ: Paulist Press, 1986), 30.

3. I considered including a traditional Christmas pudding recipe in this book but didn't for a few reasons: (1) an original thirteen-ingredient recipe is shockingly hard to find; (2) the pudding preparation is surprisingly complicated and time-consuming; and (3) a quick read of the recipe renders it, shall we say, unappealing. Perhaps the combo of beef suet, breadcrumbs, dried fruit, baking spices, and brandy sounds better to you than it does to me. If so, the internet is full of recipes you can try.

4. *The Book of Common Prayer* (Huntington Beach, CA: Anglican Liturgy Press, 2019), 679.

Christmas

1. *Liturgy of the Hours*, vol. 1, Responsory, Christmas Day, 405–406; Daily Prayer of the Church, 295.

2. *The Book of Common Prayer*, 624.

3. *The Book of Occasional Services*, (New York: The Church Hymnal Corporation, 1979), 95.

4. *The Book of Common Prayer*, 625.

5. *The Book of Common Prayer*, 77.

6. *The Book of Common Prayer*, 679.

Epiphany

1. C.S. Lewis, *The Last Battle* in The Chronicles of Narnia (New York: HarperCollins, 2001), 760.

2. Adele Ahlberg Calhoun, *Spiritual Disciplines Handbook: Practices That Form Us* (Downers Grove, IL: InterVarsity Press, 2015), 252.

3. Pfatteicher, *Heart of God*, 125; see Malachi 3:1.

4. *The Book of Common Prayer*, 604.

5. *The Book of Common Prayer*, 603.

Ash Wednesday

1. Holy oil is used in several of the church's sacramental practices: ordination, confirmation, baptism, and the anointing of the sick. As oil is used for anointing throughout Scripture for consecration unto the Lord, so holy oil is also used today.

2. *The Book of Common Prayer*, 544.

Lent

1. Holy Saturday concludes Lent, but a special chapter has been given to Holy Week due to its significance.

2. Paul Zeller Strodach, *The Church Year* (Philadelphia, PA: The United Lutheran Publication House, 1924), 102.

3. More on this starting on page 129.

4. Graham Cooke, *Hiddenness and Manifestation: What Is Really Happening When God Doesn't Seem to Be Present?: Part 1* (UK: Sovereign World, 2003), 13, 15.

5. John the Baptist has a large following. Mark 1:5 tells us, "And all the country of Judea and all Jerusalem were going out to [John] and were being baptized by him in the river Jordan, confessing their sins."

6. Jesus was, of course, in this very moment fully God. But as we see throughout the Old Testament, when God visibly reveals himself, it is obvious, overwhelming, and awe-inspiring (consider the experiences of Moses, Elijah, Daniel, Ezekiel, and Isaiah). Those who see him have no choice but to bow down and worship. Indeed, Christ's glory is revealed to Peter, James, and John at the transfiguration, and they are terrified (Mark 9:6). I suspect that partly what Satan is asking Jesus here is, "Don't you want people to know who you are? To prostrate themselves before you? To prove you are God? To be worshipped and adored as the Creator of heaven and earth?" And Jesus, in his humanity and his desire for love rather than fear, for true disciples over fearful minions, says, "This is not the will of my Father. This is not in keeping with his commandments." Satan responds, "Well, if you serve *me*, you can have all the worship and praise you desire." And with his "no," Jesus says, "I'm going to get that anyway, but it will be on my terms, not yours."

7. Lynne M. Baab, *Fasting: Spiritual Freedom Beyond Our Appetites* (Downers Grove, IL: InterVarsity Press, 2006), 16.

8. Stookey, *Calendar*, 84.

9. See list of practices on pages 80-81.

10. Saint Patrick, *His Confessions and Other Works,* trans. Fr. Neil Xavier O'Donoghue (Totowa, NJ: Catholic Book Publishing, 2009), 19.

11. *The Book of Common Prayer*, 627.

12. *The Book of Common Prayer*, 13.

13. *The Book of Common Prayer*, 606.

14. *The Book of Common Prayer*, 100–101.

Holy Week and the Triduum

1. Julia Gatta and Martin L. Smith, *Go in Peace* (New York: Morehouse, 2012), 31.
2. Dietrich Bonhoeffer, *Life Together* (New York: HarperCollins, 1954), 115.
3. Bonhoeffer, *Life Together*, 116.
4. *The Book of Common Prayer*, 121.
5. Please take into account the guidelines for fasting in chapter 9 and adapt this tradition as necessary for your health and well-being. If foregoing food is not an option for you, perhaps consider abstaining from meat (or another food group) or simply eating half-meals on Good Friday. If you have children, consider asking them to fast from sweets or TV (or something else reasonable) during this period.
6. *The Book of Common Prayer*, 607.
7. *The Book of Common Prayer*, 130.
8. *The Book of Common Prayer*, 608.

Easter

1. The Jewish calendar complicates things all the way around. While there's a full moon once every 29.5 days, this means that the Jewish year was only 354 days. This is twelve days short of the solar calendar, which fixes a year's length at 365.2425 days. While solar calendars correct for those decimal points by adding a day to the year every four years (a leap year), lunar calendars must add a *month* to their year for seven years in every 19-year cycle. In the third century, it was determined that for every 19-year cycle, a month would be added between the sixth and seventh months of the Jewish year (Adar and Nisan—the added month is called Adar II) during the third, sixth, eighth, eleventh, fourteenth, seventeenth, and nineteenth years. According to Benjamin Dreyfus—a physics professor at George Mason University—in an interview with *The Atlantic*: "The Jewish calendar drifts about one day later every 200 years, and so far there isn't any mechanism to correct that.... In about 6,000 years [Easter and Passover will] be fully out of sync if nothing is done to correct the Jewish calendar." (Robinson Meyer, "The Ancient Math That Sets the Date of Easter and Passover," *The Atlantic*, April 19, 2019. https://www.theatlantic.com/science/archive/2019/04/why-dont-easter-and-passover-always-line/587572/0.)
2. Stookey, *Calendar*, 55–56.
3. See page 16. See also Justo L. Gonzalez, *A Brief History of Sunday* (Grand Rapids, MI: Eerdmans, 2017), 29.
4. Gross, *Living the Christian Year*, 165.
5. N.T. Wright, *Surprised by Hope: Rethinking Heaven, the Resurrection, and the Mission of the Church* (New York: HarperCollins, 2008), 293.
6. Boone H. Porter, *Keeping the Church Year* (New York: Seabury Press, 1977), 68.
7. Jen Wilkin, *Ten Words to Live By* (Wheaton, IL: Crossway, 2021), 66.
8. Wilkin, *Ten Words to Live By*, 65.

9. Sunday worship must still be a priority for a Christian even if you cannot fully Sabbath on a Sunday—weekly participation in remembering our resurrection, in teaching, Eucharist, and fellowship, is vital to a flourishing spiritual life.

10. Peterson, *Working the Angles*, 78.

11. Peterson, *Working the Angles*, 67.

12. Stookey, *Calendar*, 73.

13. Adapted from *The Book of Occasional Services*.

14. *Parish* was a term that originally meant something like a "district." Until the Reformation, there weren't different denominational traditions—though the Eastern and Western Churches had split, they were divided geographically by world region. People wouldn't have the option of choosing to go to the local Orthodox or Catholic church. A country either followed one tradition or the other. So people just attended the church in their parish, and it was unfortunate indeed if they were assigned a terrible priest. There was no other option.

15. Jack King, "Get Dirty: 3 Reasons Why We Should Observe Rogation Days," Anglican Compass, May 24, 2019, https://anglicancompass.com/rogation-days/.

16. *The Book of Common Prayer*, 365.

Ascension and Pentecost

1. Pfatteicher, *Heart of God*, 258.

2. *The Book of Common Prayer*, 61.

3. Stookey, *Calendar*, 73.

4. *The Book of Common Prayer*, 646.

5. Whitsunday could also come from "Wit" Sunday—*wit* being the old English word for wisdom. Wisdom is one of the names for the Holy Spirit.

6. *Catholic All Year*, 234.

7. *The Book of Common Prayer*, 614.

Ordinary Time

1. Andrew Peterson, *Every Moment Holy* (Nashville, TN: Rabbit Room Press, 2017), xvii.

2. Buckland, *Advent to Pentecost*, 74.

3. The Athanasian Creed (which wasn't written by Athanasius and wasn't originally considered a creed) is available online at https://www.ccel.org/creeds/athanasian.creed.html.

4. *The Book of Common Prayer*, 615.

5. Because the Church began and liturgy was substantially developed in the Northern Hemisphere, significant seasonal connections are primarily found in Northern Hemisphere climates.

6. *The Book of Common Prayer*, 634.

7. Francis Weiser, *The Holyday Book* (New York: Harcourt, Brace and Company, 1956), 172.

8. *The Book of Common Prayer*, 629.

9. Tertullian, *De Corona,* "3" "At every forward step and movement, at every going in and out, when we put on our clothes and shoes, when we bathe, when we sit at table, when we light the lamps, on couch, on seat, in all the ordinary actions of daily life, we trace upon the forehead the sign."

10. *The Book of Common Prayer*, 631.

11. *The Book of Common Prayer*, 632.

12. Pfatteicher, *Heart of God*, 296.

13. *The Book of Common Prayer*, 623.

14. *The Book of Common Prayer*, 23.

15. *The Book of Common Prayer,* 50.

Allhallowtide

1. Calhoun, *Spiritual Disciplines Handbook*, 59.

2. Robert A. Davis, "Escaping Through Flames: Halloween as a Christian Festival" in *Treat or Trick? Halloween in a Globalising World*, ed. Malcolm Foley and Hugh O'Donnell (Newcastle upon Tyne: Cambridge Scholars Publishing, 2009), 39-40.

3. Mary Reed Newland, *The Year and Our Children* (Manchester, NH: Sophia Institute Press, 2007), 297.

4. *The Book of Common Prayer*, 640.

5. *The Book of Common Prayer*, 622.

6. Ben Jeffries, "A Reformed Litany of the Saints: For All Saints' Day," The North American Anglican, October 29, 2019, https://northamanglican.com/a-reformed-litany-of-the-saints-for-all-saints-day/.

BIBLIOGRAPHY

Baab, Lynne M. *Fasting: Spiritual Freedom Beyond Our Appetites*. Downers Grove, IL: InterVarsity Press, 2006.

Black, Vicki K. *Welcome to the Church Year*. Harrisburg, PA: Morehouse Publishing, 2004.

Bonhoeffer, Dietrich. *Life Together*. New York: HarperCollins Publishers, 1954.

Book of Common Prayer, The. Huntington Beach, CA: Anglican Liturgy Press, 2019.

Bradshaw, Paul F., and Maxwell E. Johnson. *The Origins of the Feasts, Fasts, and Seasons in Early Christianity*. Collegeville, MN: Liturgical Press, 2011.

Buckland, Patricia B. *Advent to Pentecost: A History of the Christian Year*. Wilton, Connecticut: Morehouse-Barlow Co., Inc., 1979.

Calhoun, Adele Ahlberg. *Spiritual Disciplines Handbook: Practices That Form Us*. Downers Grove: InterVarsity Press, 2015.

Cooke, Graham. *Hiddenness and Manifestation: What Is Really Happening When God Doesn't Seem to Be Present?: Part 1*. Lancaster, UK: Sovereign World, 2003.

Curtis, Gemma. "Your Life in Numbers," Dreams, April 28, 2021, https://www.dreams .co.uk/sleep-matters-club/your-life-in-numbers-infographic.

Dillard, Annie. *The Writing Life*. New York: HarperCollins, 1989.

English Standard Version Bible. Wheaton, IL: Crossway, 2001.

Gatta, Julia, and Martin L. Smith. *Go In Peace*. New York: Morehouse Publishing, 2012.

Gonzalez, Justo L. *A Brief History of Sunday*. Grand Rapids, MI: Eerdmans, 2017.

Gross, Bobby. *Living the Christian Year*. Downers Grove, IL: InterVarsity Press, 2009.

Guite, Malcolm. *Waiting on the Word*. Norwich, UK: Canterbury Press, 2015.

Ireton, K.C. *Circle of the Seasons: Meeting God in the Church Year*. Downers Grove, IL: InterVarsity Press, 2008.

King, Jack. "Get Dirty: 3 Reasons Why We Should Observe Rogation Days." Anglican Compass, May 24, 2019, https://anglicancompass.com/rogation-days/.

Lewis, C.S. *The Last Battle*. The Chronicles of Narnia. New York: HarperCollins, 2001.

Luther, Martin. *Luther's Small Catechism*. Lindenhurst, NY: Great Christian Books, 2013.

Newland, Mary Reed. *The Year and Our Children*. Manchester, NH: Sophia Institute Press, 2007.

Pelikan, Jaroslav. *The Vindication of Tradition: The 1983 Jefferson Lecture in the Humanities*. New Haven, CT: Yale University Press, 1984.

Peterson, Andrew. *Every Moment Holy*. Nashville, TN: Rabbit Room Press, 2017.

Peterson, Eugene H. *Eat This Book*. Grand Rapids, MI: Eerdmans, 2006.

Peterson, Eugene H. *Working the Angles*. Grand Rapids, MI: Eerdmans, 1987.

Pfatteicher, Philip H. *Journey into the Heart of God: Living the Liturgical Year*. New York: Oxford University Press, 2013.

Porter, Boone H. *Keeping the Church Year*. New York: Seabury Press, 1977.

Meyer, Robinson. "The Ancient Math That Sets the Date of Easter and Passover." *The Atlantic*, April 19, 2019. https://www.theatlantic.com/science/archive/2019/04/why-dont-easter-and-passover-always-line/587572/.

Silesius, Angelus. *The Cherubinic Wanderer*. Translated by Maria Shrady. Mahwah, NJ: Paulist Press, 1986.

Smith, James K.A. *You Are What You Love*. Grand Rapids, MI: Brazos Press, 2016.

Stookey, Laurence Hull. *Calendar: Christ's Time for the Church*. Nashville, TN: Abingdon Press, 1996.

Strodach, Paul Zeller. *The Church Year.* Philadelphia, PA: The United Lutheran Publication House, 1924.

Saint Patrick. *His Confessions and Other Works.* Translated by Fr. Neil Xavier O'Donoghue. Totowa, NJ: Catholic Book Publishing, 2009.

Tierney, Kendra. *The Catholic All Year Compendium: Liturgical Living for Real Life.* San Francisco: Ignatius Press, 2018.

Underhill, Evelyn. *Worship.* New York: The Crossroad Publishing Company, 1936.

Weiser, Francis X. *Handbook of Christian Feasts and Customs.* New York: Harcourt, Brace, and Company, 1958.

Wilkin, Jen. *Ten Words to Live By.* Wheaton, IL: Crossway, 2021.

Wright, N.T. *Surprised by Hope: Rethinking Heaven, the Resurrection, and the Mission of the Church.* New York: HarperCollins, 2008.

INDEX

POETRY CREDITS

ABOUT THE AUTHOR

Danielle Hitchen longs for people to see and understand God's big story in the everyday world around them. She is enthusiastic about church history and tradition, mental and emotional health, and living the good life. By day, Danielle is a reluctant homeschool mom, acceptable homemaker, and longtime associate producer of the *Hugh Hewitt Show*. In her spare time, she is also the author of the Baby Believer book series, founder of Catechesis Books, and occasional writer of other things (like this book). Danielle loves good stories, big ideas, and beautiful design. She and her husband live near Washington, DC, where they can be found enjoying Smithsonians and playgrounds with their three children, good conversations with their friends, and Virginia vineyards with each other.

www.CatechesisBooks.com

Published in association with the literary agency of Wolgemuth & Associates

Cover design by Studio Gearbox
Interior design by Janelle Coury
Illustrations by Stephen Crotts
Author photo by Jamie Sutera Photography

For bulk, special sales, or ministry purchases, please call 1-800-547-8979. Email: Customerservice@hhpbooks.com

SACRED SEASONS

Copyright © 2023 by Danielle Hitchen
Art copyright © 2023 by Stephen Crotts
Published by Harvest House Publishers
Eugene, Oregon 97408
www.harvesthousepublishers.com

ISBN 978-0-7369-8617-5 (hardcover)
ISBN 978-0-7369-8618-2 (eBook)

Library of Congress Control Number: 2022948978

Printed in China

23 24 25 26 27 28 29 30 31 / RDS / 10 9 8 7 6 5 4 3 2 1